Unstoppable Day

The Morning Routine to Eliminate Procrastination and Boost Productivity. No Miracles Just Pure Self-Discipline. See the Effects In 3 Days

Brendon T. Walker

© **Copyright 2019 - All rights reserved.**

The content contained within this book may not be reproduced, duplicated or transmitted without direct written permission from the author or the publisher.

Under no circumstances will any blame or legal responsibility be held against the publisher, or author, for any damages, reparation, or monetary loss due to the information contained within this book. Either directly or indirectly.

Legal Notice:

This book is copyright protected. This book is only for personal use. You cannot amend, distribute, sell, use, quote or paraphrase any part, or the content within this book, without the consent of the author or publisher.

Disclaimer Notice:

Please note the information contained within this document is for educational and entertainment purposes only. All effort has been executed to present accurate, up to date, and reliable, complete information. No warranties of any kind are declared or implied. Readers acknowledge that the author is not engaging in the rendering of legal, financial, medical or professional advice. The content within this book has been derived from various sources. Please consult a licensed professional before attempting any techniques outlined in this book.

By reading this document, the reader agrees that under no circumstances is the author responsible for any losses, direct or indirect, which are incurred as a result of the use of information contained within this document, including, but not limited to, — errors, omissions, or inaccuracies.

Contents

Introduction _____ 1

Chapter 1:
The Foundation of Success _____ 5

Chapter 2:
Fundamental Key to Daily Self-Discipline _____ 16

Chapter 3:
Habits of the Disciplined _____ 30

Chapter 4:
Surprising Mind Tricks to Master Self-Discipline ____ 40

Chapter 5:
The Secrets to Resist Temptation _____ 50

Chapter 6:
Break the Cycle Holding You Back _____ 59

Chapter 7:
Getting Work Done Even if You're Lazy _____ 69

Chapter 8:
Why You Need a Long-Term Morning Routine _____ 78

Chapter 9:
How to Multiply Your Time _____ 88

Chapter 10:
The Science Behind Why You Procrastinate _____ 94

Chapter 11:
Defeat Procrastinating with Your Mind _____ 104

Chapter 12:
The Growth Mindset Think Long-Term_____ 109

Chapter 13:
Shape Your Future _____ 116

Chapter 14:
Eat Something You Hate _____ 121

Conclusion _____ 125

UNSTOPPABLE DAY

THE MORNING ROUTINE TO ELIMINATE PROCRASTINATION AND BOOST PRODUCTIVITY. NO MIRACLES JUST PURE SELF-DISCIPLINE. SEE THE EFFECTS IN 3 DAYS

BRENDON T. WALKER

Introduction

Self-transformation is a hell of a mouthful in this generation where everything is ruled over by technology. We wake up in the morning and our first activity is to check our Facebook page for any updates. Next, we tweet about the first thing that comes into our minds such as, "Dreamed about having a house party. Want to make it a reality?" As if it ends there, we post an Instagram update of an early selfie with a caption, "Woke up Like This" and have our friends like it. At eleven, instead of cooking a fully-cooked meal, we prefer to order take out and post a Facebook update that says, "Brunch from McDonald's be like" and have our followers fawning over burger and fries.

In the afternoon, we would sulk on our couches watching Netflix until 5 pm, where our nightlife starts. We call our friends about plans and gimmicks at the club and meet there at around 7 pm. From there, we dance our feet off, chugging cases of beers, and drinking cocktails until midnight. We would spend the whole night having fun, telling stories, and just hanging out. Only to wake up and repeat the cycle the next day.

See, I think there is nothing wrong with that routine. I believe it actually is fun to be with friends whom we call "family." It maintains our youthful existence. It keeps the hype up in our lives. That's what people call "Living Life to the Fullest." Who would not want to experience such a thing?

Personally, I believe that it is a healthy lifestyle **IF YOU WANT TO REMAIN UNSUCCESSFUL IN LIFE**. Yes, partying and procrastinating is a good way to preserve youth and happiness, but for how long? I hate to be blunt, but money is a temporary commodity unless it is used in a productive way. So, what if your parents have loads of money? So, what if you are the heir of a big company? That does not mean you can do whatever you can with your assets. Think of it this way, what if your so-called company went bankrupt and your parents cannot support you anymore? What will you do by then? Sulk in your couch the whole day, waiting for apples to fall into your mouth? Even apple trees die if not taken care of properly.

Unsuccessful people look at prestigious individuals saying, "That is no big deal. They had lots of money to start their business. It is no surprise their company would grow like that. Besides, they had someone on the inside. They have it all figured out." Just like you, they might have been someone's successor as well. But even so, their journey to becoming successful was not easy. It took them years of hard work to even deserve to be a successor.

Unstoppable Day

There are others out there who literally started from rags to riches. They grew up in a third-world country where houses are made of boxes and scrap materials. Some of them started as garbage men and steel collectors. They did not have the resources to reach high school. Nevertheless, that did not stop them. Most of them already have their own line of bag and dress designs. Some of them became celebrities, showcasing their talents all around the world. Those poor individuals who were bullied and discriminated have their own company, providing jobs to thousands of people in their country. What is their secret to prestige?

If you compare your status to that of the poor, aspiring people mentioned above, you are 100 steps ahead towards success. You have a stable roof over your head. They only have garbage bags as roofing. You eat three times a day, with an allowance that can buy you everything you want. The poor people out there only eat once. Sometimes, their meals barely even touch the linings of their stomach. You were able to study and acquire a college degree, they barely reached primary education. Despite all of that has been given to you, all you do is complain and ask for more. Out of the billions of people in this world, you are part of the lucky 20% who does not experience poverty. You have everything you need to reach success if you wanted to. So, what do they have that you do not?

Courage, Persistence, and Inspiration. These three words kept them going despite everything they do not have. These words kept them alive. It allowed them to rise from the line of poverty and reach their dreams as they moved forward. Because of these three words, they were able to send their nine siblings to college. These three words gave them the power to look past their differences and persevere towards success.

If you are wondering how these three words alone brought them success, it all goes back to the most important trait: SELF-DISCIPLINE. Those poor people could have chosen to procrastinate and remain stagnant. Instead, they thrived in the depths of poverty and seized every opportunity to survive. They could have chosen to feel helpless and sorry to be born and die in poverty, but no, they chose to change their lives. Simply put, it was all about mind over matter - A concept that 20% of the world seems to disregard.

Controlling the mind can do wonders to your life. With self-discipline, you can survive your worst nightmares. You can thrive in the midst of your hardest battles. You can rise from the depths of the hell you are going through. All you need to do is keep in mind the three words that will bring you to success: COURAGE, PERSISTENCE, AND INSPIRATION. Not only will you transform into a powerful being, but also reach a paradise you once deemed impossible to achieve.

Chapter 1:
The Foundation of Success

We all know that "Determination is the key to success." And with determination come our three big words: Persistence, Courage, and Inspiration. Everyone has what it takes to develop these characteristics over time, yet only a few reaches their ultimate goal. Why is that? Simply because most people disregard the trait that roots all values. The one word that encompasses the definitive morale that leads to success – SELF-DISCIPLINE. It should not be "Determination" as the key to a prestigious life, but "Self-discipline" itself. Without it, persistence, courage, and inspiration -among other values- will cease to exist.

Self-discipline is the value of persistent self-control. It is the ability to stick to your decisions and goals, learning to say "no," and obtaining full command of your mind and body. Self-discipline entails focus, control, and restraint to overcome even the most enticing temptation in life. In other words, self-discipline is the power of mind-mastery. It is the ability to take control of your mind and not be a slave to it. Do you know why millions of people aspire, yet only a few of them succeed? Because people speak of self-discipline as if they know so much about it but, when it comes to its application, it is way easier said than done. People have a lot of perceptions as to what drives a person to succeed. Some say passion, others say hard work. Truth is, all of these values mean nothing without self-control. SELF-DISCIPLINE is the mother of all values. It magnifies the ability to elicit and emancipate the necessary values to succeed. In this chapter, we will dig deep on the qualities that drive a person to success, and explain why SELF-DISCIPLINE is the true foundation to success.

Every dreamer is like a painter. First, they envision their creation before they engage on the verge of artistry. On the road to success.

Motivation drives a person to move forward. It serves as the blank canvass where we visualize and craft our dreams and aspirations, giving us guidelines on what our future can look like. Motivation is the cognitive appraisal of a reward that feels like success. It gives us a reason to work hard and persevere against all adversities. Whether the reward is extrinsic -such as wealth and fame- or intrinsic -such as honor and happiness- a person's motivation provides inspiration to thrive despite hardships and challenges.

A lot of situations can deter us from our motivation. Sometimes, we get tired of putting so much effort into our dreams and we start to lose hope. We start to lose sight of what it means to succeed. We start to dissuade ourselves from ever moving forward because all we see in front of us is a dead end.

Unstoppable Day

On the road to success, never expect to have few trials. In real life, we face a daily skirmish with our minds, our hearts, and our society. There is a never-ending search for goals and meaning. All you need to do is develop the art of not giving up. Developing a good sense of self-discipline will allow a person to look past the challenges and focus on the prize ahead. It keeps the vision straight and crystal clear. See, motivation is not only an impetus towards success, but it is also a conduit towards positive thinking. Self-discipline will push you to look past the negativities and have a more positive perception of everything.

Courage is the first step we take before our real trials begin. The journey begins once we discover our audacity to engage in different life battles. Trust me, life will beat you down and take a little bit of your soul every day. Courage allows you to walk past the pain and agony and learn from your mistakes. Life will test your bravery. It will make you face your deepest and darkest fears. At this stage, every step you take seems to lead into a pit where none of your dreams will survive.

But with self-discipline, you convince yourself: "No, I will not yield from your challenges. Should I fail, I will rise up and conquer all trials and live my dream to its fullest." We know for sure there are battles we cannot win. In turn, self-discipline teaches the mind to take it on anyway. It is not about overcoming challenges but learning from them instead. That is the key. courage should not be only at the beginning.

We should muster bravery consistently even after we have reached our goals. There is no end in learning, which is why we should be brave enough to tackle every challenge and gain more wisdom as time goes by. Developing self-discipline helps you be bolder. You need to face all the trials in life. There is so much bravery in learning from your mistakes. It pushes you to keep your head up high no matter how hard life has beaten you down.

Determination means being purposeful to overcome all challenges in life. You stick to your plan and stay focused on your goal no matter what it costs. As you begin your journey towards success, trials will be inevitable. Some challenges will cause you to lose your sense of purpose, diminish your spirit, and break your intent towards your dreams. Without self-discipline, it is easy to give in to pressure.

I once knew a person who wanted to be a successful psychologist. She wanted to build her own clinic and make a name for herself as a successful therapist. She wanted to provide a home for the mentally disabled and teach them practical habits of survival. For four years in college, she was determined to study hard to pass the board exams. This way, she would be one step closer to her dreams. When she graduated, it was difficult for her to find a job suitable for her course. Her parents disapproved of her career choice, so they kept convincing her to find another line of work. Her parents always wanted her to be an accountant because of the salary. One of her uncles was willing to send her back to finish an accountancy degree, but she was

Unstoppable Day

a very determined woman. That is what I admired about her. Despite the pressure her parents put upon her, she stuck to her goal and passed the Psychology Board Exams. Now, she is a well-known psychotherapist who has provided shelter to hundreds of mentally incapacitated people and given job opportunities to aspiring psychologists. She could not have done it without her rock-solid determination.

With a tiny bit of self-discipline, your determination will be unstoppable. None of those hindrances will be strong enough to break your meaning and purpose in life.

Commitment is vital to success as well. This pertains to a person's dedication to his or her goal. Commitment or dedication causes a person to uphold his responsibilities and duties no matter how difficult it is to accomplish them. On the road to success, life will test your commitment to your goals. For example, you want to build a business by investing in your skills. Being committed to your goal means facing any adversity to make your dreams happen. This includes holding yourself liable for any profit or loss incurred in during the process.

A lot of people out there are skeptical about starting a business. Sure, it is a good way to earn money, but people only see how risky it is. It entails a regular, in-depth analysis of both the market and economy. Starting a business is a trial-and-error method of which services or products to introduce. It involves strategic advertising and promotion to establish a name and gather customers. Business includes risking a huge amount of capital, hoping it can generate income, and not incur in a loss. The steps we take towards success are straight-up terrifying and dangerous. These challenges can and will test your commitment but, with self-discipline, no amount of fear can dissuade you from pursuing what you love. It commands you to keep moving forward despite the losses. It pushes you to keep trying until you succeed in your chosen line. With self-discipline, no amount of liability will make you lose sight of your goals. No amount of burden will derail you from being committed to your dreams.

Time Management is better known as self-management because it is the ability to organize -and carry out- your activities. It also refers to the establishment of sync between your mind and body. You are not actually managing the time of day. You are handling yourself to establish a productive body clock to accomplish your tasks as scheduled. Self-management refers to the balance between rest and effort without procrastinating. Without this coordination, no agenda will push through, leaving you in the depths of lethargy and stagnation.

The most notorious enemy of self-management is procrastination. When continuous effort causes burnout and fatigue, the mind and body start to wear off. When this happens, all you want to do is sleep all day and think of nothing else but relaxation. However, too much rest is detrimental to progress, since it leads to unproductiveness. Do not underestimate how tempting temporary idleness can be. Never

Unstoppable Day

listen to your mind when it tells you, "Fifteen minutes on Facebook will not hurt." Minutes turn to hours. Hours (can) turn to days. When your mind and body start to procrastinate, it is a very difficult place to come back from, which is why self-discipline is a necessary trick against lazy days. It sets your body on alarm, preventing it from giving in to procrastination. If you plan to rest, set an alarm and condition your mind to rest for a few minutes before you get back to work.

Time-management is a major factor in leading a successful life. Even so, without self-discipline, your system and schedule will turn into a lost cause. Body and mind conditioning revert back to zero. Precious time is wasted. And all your efforts will soon be undone. To maintain a stable mindset towards success, always develop your sense of self-discipline. It commands your brain towards consistency. It allows you to defer from distractions and efficiently walk a straight line on the road to success.

Willpower. It allows for self-reliance and independence to flow on a person's veins. It teaches the mind there is nobody else to rely on but oneself. With the streak of independence coursing through your actions, your decisions are your command. Your actions are made out of your own will. No other person can tell you what to do or how to live your life.

However, there are challenges that can put your willpower to the test. Sometimes, we feel like things are getting out of control and we can no longer do anything about it. It may seem that fate is doing an intervention, telling us our dream is not meant to be. Don't despair. This so-called destiny is a mind-driven concept. Wherever you are now, it's a consequence of your past actions and decisions. If you decide to keep on living towards your dream, then *that* will be your destiny. No hardship or "signs" from the universe will tell you otherwise. With willpower, you have the strength to break the hands of destiny and walk your own path. You should not burden yourself with common sayings such as "If it is meant to be, it will be" because if you really want something to work, you will do everything in your power to make sure it does. Not even destiny will be able to stop you.

Self-discipline plays a key role in your consistent will to reach your goals. Without self-discipline, your mind will start to doubt your dreams and you will give in to your fears. Your mind will be inclined to listen to criticism that will derail you off your tracks. If you really are determined to reach your dreams, focus on your decisions. Learn from your mistakes. Never let it detract your focus and lose sight of the prize.

Passion refers to the emotion you put into your work. It is your zeal, your emotion and your enthusiasm that leads to success. Passion brings fire into your life. It boosts up your fervor and magnifies your power. Passion is the love you have for your work; it is what drives you into doing whatever it takes to succeed. Without passion, your life would feel like an improvised prison. Success will feel more like a burden rather than an inspiration. Every accomplishment will seem more like an encumbrance rather than a blessing. On the road towards success, it is important to keep passion flowing. Not only does it spark confidence, but determination and persistence as well.

Of course, your passion will be challenged plenty of times, but you need to remember why you loved your work in the first place. Remind yourself how it makes you feel. Remember the great moments that brought learning and growth. In doing so, your passion will ignite a never-ending motivation, giving way to change in your life. Self-discipline -along with passion- will make you unstoppable in reaching your dreams. Self-discipline will train your mind not to lose hope despite any circumstances. It will show you how to maintain a burning love and zeal towards your line of work. With these two values combined, nothing can stop you from achieving the success you deserve.

Confidence and self-discipline form a very effective combination. People always tell you to "believe in yourself" in order to achieve your goals. Thing is, it's very difficult to follow that motto when in self-doubt. It is common knowledge that confidence refers to your belief that you can accomplish a task or a goal. It is your faith that YOU CAN DO IT! Self-confidence is your assurance of your own skill set and intellect. Confidence is an important way to master boldness and face your trials. However, too much of it can cause your timely undoing. As human beings, there is always room for improvement. We will always have weaknesses in line with our strengths, which is why there should be a balance between humility and confidence. Crossing the line into overconfidence can lead to great peril on your road to success. Overconfidence inhibits your ability to reflect in your abilities and acknowledge your mistakes. It gives way to greed and avarice, characteristics that have doomed millions of entrepreneurs to failure.

Confidence powered by self-discipline will allow you to keep track of your behavior. It prevents a lack of confidence and self-doubt. In turn, it inhibits your mind from being too arrogant and greedy when making decisions. It signals your mind not to enter the depths of overconfidence. It sends out an alarm saying, "Whoops, aren't you a bit out of your head? Humble yourself up a little and reflect on your real skills. Stop being so greedy." Self-discipline maintains the normal threshold of diffidence a person can have.

Integrity is one of the most important values of mankind. It means being trustworthy and honest to other people. It is about having a good moral compass or choosing the right way rather than the easy one. Integrity brings honor and decency to an individual. It pushes us to make noble and righteous decisions. To achieve pure happiness in life, a person must uphold his integrity over others. Success out of mischief and deceit never lasts long. Sure, it can get you out of problems, and probably get you more money, but those means of action will eventually come back to haunt you and drag you back to the depths of your own hell.

Unstoppable Day

On the road to success, you will face issues that challenge your commitment to integrity. These problems will tear your willpower apart, doubt your existence, and influence your actions. Eventually, you will get tired of all the righteousness and morality you uphold in our decisions, but this should not stop you from doing the right thing. With self-discipline, you can withstand any temptation that goes your way. With a proper mindset, you can ward off any influence that dooms your decisions into treachery or any other forms of immorality. If you develop and maintain self-discipline, you can uplift your spirit into doing what's right. As long as you know your conscience is clean, you will find no setback that can pull you out of the road to success.

Chapter 2:
Fundamental Key to Daily Self-Discipline

"If you want to live a happy life, tie it to a goal, not to people or things."

Albert Einstein

I grew up in a society where beauty, health, and fitness matters. Social media has created a definition of what is attractive, sexy, and intelligent. In this modern world, beauty means being white and blemish-free. Sexiness is defined as having a Coca-Cola shaped figure. Intelligence means taking a course in engineering, accountancy, teaching, or architecture. The rest is subject to bullying and criticism. When my cousin Liddy was a teenager, her classmates and neighbors kept making fun of her because of her body. Ever since she was a kid, she had a very slow metabolism. No matter how much she engaged in weight-loss activities, nothing worked. Eventually, she just stopped trying and disappeared into a pit of helplessness. This made her a victim of body-shaming and bullying on campus. As she grew up, she became very desperate to lose weight and have a "sexy" figure. She was envious of the girls who seemed carefree in maintaining their weight and figure.

Unstoppable Day

I watched her try every trick in the book, including carb cutting and workout, but nothing really worked. One Monday morning, I decided to keep her company at 5:30 to jog around the city. I was really excited to see our fellow fitness enthusiasts. To my surprise, at 5:30 in the morning, we saw businessmen walking to and from the streets. Liddy and I stared at each other in disbelief. Offices did not open for at least another 2 hours. How come people were already suited for work? As we jogged further, we overheard a fellow fitness enthusiast talking with a suited man, "Done with your routine?" he asked, and the suited man gave him a quick high-five and passed on. Could it be that at 6:00 in the morning these businessmen had already done their early morning workout and got ready for work? I mean, how do they do that? I can even barely wake up at 4 AM, much less finish working out at 5.

Could it be that these daily routines play a role in becoming a fit and successful entrepreneur?

For many years, I have observed and studied the habits of the successful. I have concocted my own surveys on how those entrepreneurs get to finish their workout at 5 AM and be on their business attires 30 minutes after that. After months of continuous learning, I have determined the most important value: SELF-DISCIPLINE. This time, not only will it lead to success, but overall life-transformation as well.

Over the course of my life, I have watched as my cousins tried different weight-loss activities and lose hope as time went by, going back to their old habits. Because of this, I realized that successful weight loss is not about diet or strenuous exercise, it is about commitment and faith laced with long-term self-discipline. My cousins never intended to follow a diet or training program after a month without improvements. This repressed their ability to keep pushing themselves to the limit. The process is the same when striving for prestige and success. It is not always about the decisions and actions you take, but the commitment and faith you put into your work. These two values lead a person towards a holistic life transformation, including physical, emotional, and psychological development.

Earlier, we discussed the relationship of commitment and confidence to self-discipline. In this chapter, I will talk about the five fundamental steps to a long-term self-transformation – the conduit towards goal achievement.

The Fundamental Steps to Self-Transformation
These five steps towards self-transformation will allow you to acquire a higher level of self-discipline. Soon thereafter, you will realize that every other value, such as commitment and confidence, will follow suit. These steps do wonders for your physical development and will start to hone your psychological and emotional strength as well.

But why should you need psychological and emotional strength if your only target is weight loss? Well, I personally believe that every person has the inclination to achieve self-actualization or the fulfillment of one's potential and finding the meaning of life. Everyone has the need to rise from the depths of being a 'nobody' to becoming the 'somebody' this world needs. Developing long-term self-discipline will allow you to do just that. Before you start following the steps below, you must know that self-transformation is not an overnight thing. Sometimes, it takes two to three years before it can be attained. Trust me when I tell you it will be worth the wait. The self-transformation you gain through commitment and self-confidence will emancipate you until your last breath. For this, I want you to promise yourself to stay committed to your goals and actions. I want you to believe in yourself, to believe that you can do it. Take courage to start and finish your milestones without having any kind of self-doubt.

Without further ado, here are the Fundamental Steps to a Successful Self-Transformation:

Establish a Vision
First, I want you to think about your body, career, relationship, family or financial goals. Or anything that matters in your life. Visualize what you want to happen. Describe it detail by detail. If it helps, you can jot those down on a piece of paper or a notebook and hold on to it for dear life. I want you to imagine what it would be like to have the sexy body you always dreamed of. Picture your dream partner reaching

towards you. What is he like? What do you have in common? What about your career? What do you really want to do in life? Do you want to be stuck reading and shredding the same number of papers every day or do you want to achieve something greater? How huge do you want your salary or income to be? Do you want to stick to the low-grade salary you always get at the end of the month or do you want to raise your commission? Think about your family. If you have kids, think about their future. What do you want it to look like? What would your plans for your parents be by then? Where –or how- will you spend vacation with them in five to ten years' time?

See, this vision that I want you to develop is the motivation to keep going no matter happens. It is your drive, your prize, your inspiration to move forward through all adversities. I want you to write it all in a journal in deep detail. If it helps, you can sketch out your dream body, dream house, and dream car.

In the morning when you wake up, and at night before you go to bed, I want you to rethink your dreams and aspirations. Remind yourself why you want self-transformation. Visit your journal and reread what you want in life. To keep you focused on your goals later on, I want you to never lose sight of that promise you made to yourself. In a way of helping, you can create your own mantra and focus on it, such as, "I will achieve my dreams only if I will allow it," or "I can do anything as long as I believe." Small as these actions are, they help you become unstoppable.

Create A Plan of Action

Your plan of action is the long-term milestone you want to carry out. However, this can be very hard to accomplish without a stable sense of self-identity. SELF-IDENTITY or SELF-CONCEPT is a very important factor for a realistic goal-setting. It defines how much you know yourself, how you perceive yourself, and how you present yourself to challenges. Without a good sense of self-identity, establishing an attainable plan of action is impossible. Too much self-appraisal can cause depression, anxiety, and other mental health-related issues. Too little self-appreciation can diminish self-worth and repress your strength, all of which are crucial to establishing a life-long self-transformation goal.

Creating a plan of action requires knowing yourself from the inside and out. To set your short-term goals later on, you need to know your strengths, weaknesses, opportunities, and threats. You must analyze what you need and what you can provide. On the aspects you mentioned above, I want you to do a SWOT (Strengths, Weaknesses, Opportunities, and Threats) Analysis in relation to each one of them.

For example, on your journey to weight loss, you have an opportunity to join the gym and hire an instructor. However, the threat is that you own a pastry shop and it is hard to say no to the good stuff. In your career, you can indicate your skill set as your strengths, and identify your fear of giving up the position as a weakness. On your opportunities, indicate whether there is a chance for promotion or any other jobs offered with a greater salary. The only probable threat is, "What if I do not get the job, what will I do then?"

Deal with Adversities
Seeing your weaknesses on that SWOT Analysis table can be pretty devastating. It causes self-doubt and erodes your confidence. However, in this step, you will learn how to deal with various adversities, walk past the negativities, and regain your confidence once again.

Acknowledge your Weakness. Everyone has their own weaknesses, but this should not get in the way of leading a successful life. Before you feel dissuaded into pursuing your dream, remember, you do not have the worst weakness in the world. Other people cannot even get out of their houses because of Agoraphobia, or the irrational fear of being helpless in public places. But even these people do not get discouraged by their phobia. On their road to success, they put triple efforts on their recovery just to regain their functionality as a person. So, if you think you have the biggest issues, think again. Whatever situation you are in, there is always a fixture to keep you going. All you need to do is accept your weaknesses and acknowledge them as a part of you. Once you have embraced your weaknesses wholeheartedly, you will be more inclined to face the adversities that your weaknesses will give way to.

Remind yourself of its Temporariness. The most permanent thing in this world is change. Much like adversities, we solve a challenge for a day just to wake up and face another one, but as you walk along the road to success, you will realize that all adversities are temporary. You are faced with different problems each day. Some are more difficult than others, but still, they teach you different lessons. These life trials eventually pass, sometimes even on their own. What you need to do is have a little bit of confidence and courage to face each day with a burning passion and will. Remind yourself you have tackled worse problems than what you are confronting now. Think about the times when you almost broke down and turned your back on your goals but didn't because you believed in yourself. Look where it got you. See, these challenges are a normal part of life. Everyone experiences them to learn, grow, and develop. If you acknowledge problems as a part of life, nothing can dissuade you from aiming for that goal with all your strength.

Learn from Others. You do not have to be alone when dealing with adversities. Sometimes, we need other people's assistance to teach us how to overcome the challenges we face in the pursuit of our dreams. If you want to lose weight, join the gym and ask for an instructor. If you want to learn some skills, approach someone who can teach you. If you want to be a successful entrepreneur, learn from the actions of successful businessmen and imitate what they did to gain prestige.

Believe in Success. Our trials in life can keep us from reaching further. Sometimes, we feel hopeless, helpless, and desperate in our path to success. Time will come when we would eventually feel like all our actions are useless and all our dreams are impossible to fulfill. To keep your confidence burning under your skin, look for people who have successfully reached their life milestones. Read stories that can inspire you to keep pushing yourself to the limit. Remind yourself your dream is possible because, if they could do it, you just have to believe you can do it better.

Some people came from poor families but were able to transcend from that status and rise up to be successful entrepreneurs. They had literally nothing but commitment and confidence. Look at your current status: you have a roof over your head, a comfortable bed to sleep on and eat three times a day. You have everything you need to magnify your strength. If the only thing stopping you is self-doubt, take a look at the people who you admire the most. Where did they come from? Where did they start? Now, look at yourself in the mirror. You have clean clothes on your back and a penny in your pocket. That's when you realize you have more than what they started with.

Do you want to redefine the meaning of impossible? Think of them. Let their success stories be an inspiration to drive your confidence on the road to success.

Create a Collateral. If you are still hesitant to face the adversities of life, the simple thing to do is focus on your threats ahead of time and plan a collateral for them. If you really want to overcome the challenges you encounter when sprinting towards your goals, plan how to beat them with many days to spare. For example, if you want to lose weight and run a pastry shop at the same time, you must learn to say "No, thank you." The pastry is not your enemy. *You* are the impending threat. Your mind will tempt you to look at how delicious those goods are, but you need to be strong enough to commit to your diet and say *No*. Of course, the first days of 'abstinence' will be the hardest thing you will have to go through. Give it a week or two. Eventually, saying no becomes your forte. Not only will you avoid the goods in your pastry shop, but any other no-no food as well.

Another example is when you plan on applying for another job but are too afraid of resigning. Then don't. If you apply for another job, keep your old job as a collateral just in case you do not get it. At least, you tried your best and did not lose anything. However, this does not mean that you will stop trying. There will be other job opportunities out there that will certainly work wonders for your career, which is why you must never stop believing.

Generate Goals

The next step towards self-transformation is setting your short-term goals according to your plan. This is the stage where strict monitoring and commitment is required. Once again, generate your short-term goals for each of the life aspects you have listed above. This time, you will need to boost your commitment to every objective you constitute.

For example, if you aim to lose weight, you need to choose and start following a diet and a workout program. Commit yourself every day and monitor your improvements as a way of motivation. Remember, discipline is the key. To establish a successful self-transformation, you need to overcome any temptation that can get you off track, or your efforts will flush themselves down the drain.

In order to gain long-term self-discipline, you can start by going one week without breaking any of your goals. This is the hardest phase of the self-transformation project. For the first step, set an alarm and schedule your workout routine and create a list of the 'dos' and 'don'ts' on your diet. Follow this routine for one to two weeks without any glitches and everything will flow like a river. Whenever you feel lazy and tempted to break it –even for a minute-, look at yourself in the mirror and repeat your mantra at least ten times. Condition your mind into believing that breaking your habit will bring you back to where you started. Remember your motivation. Remember what inspires you. Never let yourself break character. Here are five tips to maintain your daily self-transformation streak:

Remove any Form of Temptation. Wherever you go, make sure to eliminate all sources of temptation. As in the case of weight loss, make sure to remove all unhealthy food in the fridge, and exchange those with veggies, fruits, and yogurt. If you want to work without any distractions, create a workstation in a separate room without any television or gadgets to tempt you into procrastination.

Unstoppable Day

Changing does not always feel right. Self-transformation can cause positive change to look like an impending crisis. However, you should not let this stop you. Your body does not label change as something positive in the beginning. It will always feel like there is something missing. It will make you unhappy and doubt your decisions. On the road to self-transformation, you need to acknowledge the "It does not feel right" perception to avoid being misled by temptation. Keep your mind focused on your goals and never stop committing to them. Sooner or later, your body and mind will start to accept these changes and they will become a huge part of your personality.

Failure is a Part of Success. We are only human beings. We are prone to making mistakes and bad decisions. On the road to self-transformation, do not beat yourself up whenever you don't do well in a task or you do not get something right. Discipline takes practice, it cannot be mastered overnight. Whenever you fail, do not be dissuaded from moving forward. Consider all mistakes as a form of learning. Retrace your steps to what went wrong and grow from it, but never beat yourself up because of it, since it can lead to depression or anxiety, which in turn might be the cause of your dreams' demise. Learn to forgive yourself when you encounter a glitch in your way. As human beings, we fall down, all the more reason to rise back up higher.

Focus on one day at a time. As you establish your milestones on the road to self-transformation, learn to focus on the present, not the past nor the future. Putting your attention on the past will only distract you from your current goals. It reminds you of your past failures and mistakes. Do not focus on tomorrow either, as it brings stress and apprehension. Thinking about tomorrow can detract your focus on what is in store for you today. To concentrate on getting through your tasks, focus on what you need to do right now and stick to it. Do not overthink your future plans. Learn to cross the bridge when you get there. For now, think about what you can do to improve yourself even more.

Use technology wisely. At this day and age, gadgets will most certainly distract us from accomplishing our objectives. Believe me, I know there are a lot of cool and interesting apps to try out, but in order to build a fully-transformed self, you need to utilize your gadgets in accordance with your plan. There are a lot of applications that can help you lose weight. There is the daily workout reminder app, drink water app, a routine for fitness app, and many more. If your goal is to target your cognitive aspect, you can download brain training apps, reading apps, and quiz bee apps that can help you sharpen your mind. If you lack motivation, there are apps that can help you meditate or provide helpful quotes and inspirational messages.

You can also put gadgets in a different light by using them as a 'time signal' for your workout routine. If you want to watch television, do it while working out. If you want to listen to music, use each playlist as a timeline for each set. If you want to play a game, download one that can make you sweat, such as Dance Central and other body simulation games.

Get Some Rest

Cheat days are important for keeping your head in the game. Schedule one day in a week where you can do whatever you want. You can break your diet and your exercise routines, procrastinate and give into temptation. We are only human, and as such we should not be deprived of the things we love. If we are, we become prone to untimely breaks of our self-transformation habits. To ensure the development of continuous self-discipline, a break from time to time can help a person stay motivated, stay on track. Cheat days are also known as reward days. Once the brain is accustomed to a reward at the end of every week, it will be conditioned to keep putting an effort into every routine. Do not be afraid to fall back into the abyss after the cheat day. Once you start your week with another routine, you will find your commitment and confidence to be stronger. Any other setback will seem like a walk in the park.

Now that you know everything necessary to have life-long self-discipline, the last thing to do is to maintain a strong sense of commitment and confidence. These two, laced with self-control, will lead you to become one of the most successful people on Earth. Who knows, you will probably be writing your own success story in a couple of years.

Chapter 3:
Habits of the Disciplined

"Whenever you want to achieve something, keep your eyes open, concentrate and make sure you know exactly what it is you want. No one can hit their target with their eyes closed."

Paulo Coelho

Successful minds have disciplined hearts. Not only do they have control over their thinking, but they also have mastery over their emotions. These two combined create an unstoppable personality that can withstand any adversity in life. The real reason for prestige is not only sweat and blood, but also self-command. It requires practice, training, and persistence to master. No matter how much you speak of it, if you don't know how to apply it, nothing good will ever come towards you. In order to achieve self-transformation, one needs to develop the habits of the disciplined. Once a person has fully mastered these tricks, nothing will ever come in their way towards success.

A habit is something that automates your routine and runs your behavior. It allows a higher-level thinking, unstoppable focus, and an

Unstoppable Day

unrelenting persistence towards a person's decisions. A habit is something that controls your mind and vibrates into your body. Once acquired, actions will flow easily and peacefully throughout your veins.

If you are wondering how successful people figured their lives out, it all started by developing important behavioral habits. As we discussed earlier, it is important to obtain commitment and self-confidence to execute these actions successfully. Start one day at a time, practicing each one as they come along. You do not have to rush yourself into mastering these abilities. With time and practice, you will be able to carry these out without even thinking about it. Once you do, congratulate yourself, for you have achieved the first milestone towards a self-actualized personality.

Below, I have constituted ten habits of the disciplined. As you adopt these behaviors, you will realize how strong they can impact your ability to cope, understand, think, and decide. Being successful means creating change in the world. These 10 habits are your primary stepping stones into changing old habits and gaining self-discipline.

Avoid Wasting Time. First and foremost, avoid idle time. It is important to always do something productive in your day-to-day routine. Instead of being a couch potato, watching movies the whole day, try reading inspirational books to keep you going or, if you want to watch a movie, why don't you work out while you do it? Use technology wisely. Do not let it sulk you into the depths of procrastination and unproductiveness.

Successful people are uncomfortable wasting time because it is the most expensive commodity that nobody can bring back. Once time has passed, the only things left are satisfaction or regret. A person is satisfied when he knows he has done something good with his time. On the other hand, all the lazy person has is regret. At least in the long run. Yes, for a while, he had some fun, but as he grows up, he will soon realize that he should have done something good while he was young.

This generation underestimates the allure of time. People only realize how precious it is once it has already gone by. Do not be like the rest, who spend all their time on social media and playing games when you can be out there establishing your business, investing on your skills, and trying your best to become successful in life.

Focus on the Present. There is always room for improvement in a person's personality. People who say, "This is who I am. You either accept or reject me" are somewhat immature and narcissist. A person will always have room for personality development, no matter how dark or crooked his background is. On the road to Self-Transformation, one's background is not of importance. In its place, the present takes the spotlight, as you prepare for the future. The society where you came from, the abuse you have experienced, the hardships you have overcome. All that brought you to where you are now. Instead of focusing on negativities, focus on what you can do now to furnish your personality on your way to success. The past is just a setback. It reminds you that you are worthless and undeserving of happiness and success. Do not listen to those voices inside your head. Grasp it, take a hold of it and do not let it control you ever again. Your past doesn't dictate your destiny. You are the captain of your own ship, and as such, you decide where to go and what to do.

Create a Formula. If you're wondering what famous scientists like Albert Einstein, Isaac Newton, and Rene Descartes did to achieve their success and fame, let me tell you: they created their own formula. You do not have to be a scientist to make your own. All you need is a little bit of wit and creativity. Try to apply a formula in everything you do. For example, in your expenses, for every X that you earn every month, you will only spend Y. For every calorie intake -X-, you need to burn an amount -Y-.

Some people think these formulas are just mere child's play, that they don't really work. There are a lot of possibilities that can challenge this concept, but on the road to self-discipline, challenges will not be a problem because of your persistence and control. If you stick to this formula, you can use it to gain control over your actions. Who knows, maybe you will even write about it one day.

Brendon T. Walker

Be one with the Community. If you're thinking about how being one with the community can help you transform, I have the answer: you cannot learn everything on your own. By interacting with different people, you can learn a lot of values, skills, and life lessons. Being one with the community does not mean pouring your time to socialization. It just means being supportive and trustworthy, especially in the face of calamity. On your way to success, don't expect to always walk through it alone. You will always find travel buddies and companions who will help you. Being one with the community through interaction teaches three of the most important values in a team: cooperation, understanding, and reliability. To be a good leader someday, you need to be a good follower. In order to be a good follower, you need to be an effective leader.

Make the habit of socializing with other people, even if you're not comfortable. Apart from the fact that you learn from their experiences, you also muster the confidence and self-esteem to become more open to the world and more assertive in your actions. Socialization can decrease self-doubt and increase your interpersonal intelligence. Therefore, it can help you develop a healthy emotional status. It has been proven that interacting with other people, especially friends and family can reduce the risk of depression, anxiety, and other mental disorders.

Eat Healthily. Our bodies are like machines. They need healthy fuel to function properly. Remember: you are what you eat. On the path to success, you need to start choosing what you take into your body. Avoid junk and fatty food as much as possible, given that these can make your body and mind sluggish, inhibiting your ability to think, decide, and criticize your actions. Ingesting a lot of junk food and artificial sugars can impair the balance of hormones that our glands secrete. In turn, it causes physical problems such as obesity, and heart and kidney failure. Moreover, junk food can also cause psychological disturbances. Eating unhealthy foods can cause an imbalance in a person's level of serotonin, dopamine, and endorphin, which are the necessary features to feel good and happy.

Eating more fruits and vegetables can boost up your mind and provide enduring energy for your body. Once you start eating power foods and stick to the diet, you will realize the wonders it can bring to your body when it comes to physical, emotional, and psychological wellness. Depressed individuals are advised to eat nutritious food groups and avoid skipping meals. When they follow the program effectively, changes in their mindset start to occur, and they become better individuals eventually.

At first, it would be difficult to adjust your body's eating schedule, which is why you might want to set an alarm when mealtime comes. Accustom your mind to eat three times a day. It could be at 8:00 AM, Noon, and 7 PM. Remove any temptation from your refrigerator, and exchange it with healthy food. Do this for a couple of weeks, and you will find yourself to be healthier than ever.

Maintain Healthy Sleep. Sleep is important to regulate the status of your body. After a long day's work, the body experiences a lot of stress, causing an imbalance in its chemical structure. This affects our physical and psychological health. Sleep reverts the body back to homeostasis, relaxes both the mind and the body, and 'recharges' you for another stressful day. If you look closely at the people who do not get enough sleep, they are more prone to depression, anxiety, and physical illnesses. They are prone to having heart diseases and other organ failures as a result of restlessness.

If you're not used to sleeping early, force yourself to get into bed at 8:00 or 9:00 PM. Tell your mind you need to sleep so you can wake up early in the morning. Do not let your mind take control of your body. Grab a hold of your mind and command it to sleep. The first few weeks will be the hardest, but once your mind has been conditioned to sleep at those hours, you will realize that falling asleep early will not be a problem anymore. It only takes commitment and persistence to master this craft.

Exercise Regularly. Exercising regularly is a very important tool when striving for success in self-transformation. Scientists have proven that exercise can increase the levels of endorphin or "feel-good" hormones in the body. This is a must to carry out your activities for the day. It hypes up your mood and enhances your energy to have a powered mind and body to get through the day. In the previous chapter, we discussed how to schedule yourself towards regular exercises.

Unstoppable Day

Now you know that working out is not only necessary for weight loss but also necessary towards a successful Self-Transformation. This will provide balance for your body and strengthen your mind in the face of certain adversities that life can send your way.

Organize your Schedule. Managing your schedule will not make you a control freak. It just means you're strong enough to manage your time and accomplish goals for the day. Scheduling your tasks and objectives is key when going for success. It avoids idle time and reminds you of the things you need to do. Organizing your schedule means living on your body clock. To accomplish this, you will need self-control and commitment. For example, if you take long showers, you must reverse that habit by setting yourself on alarm. If you want to take a shower at about 8 o'clock in the evening, set a 15-minute timer. Once it goes off, you should get out of the bathroom and get dressed. Another example: if you take too long to eat, schedule you're eating period for about 15 minutes for every meal. In the morning, schedule your meal from 8:00 to 8:15, 12:00 to 12:15 at noon, and 7:00 to 7:15 in the evening. For TV, gaming, and social media enthusiasts out there, you can create your schedule to limit your use of all your gadgets as well. For example, to decrease the number usage hours, set your game time, TV time, or social media time for one hour. Once the timer goes off, move to more productive activities.

Maintain a clean environment. How can a clean environment help in self-transformation? Well, within this is a very important factor to boost the mind, body, and soul. Clutters and garbage can impede the mind from thinking smoothly. As the old saying goes, your actions imitate your thoughts. If your things are scattered, it could mean your mind is scattered as well. This could indicate a lack of focus and concentration on your plans and activities. Psychologists have linked the cleanliness of a workspace or work environment to optimal performance. Specialists have also found that uncleanliness is directly correlated to mental illnesses and physical diseases.

Now, if you were to ask me, "This is my personality. It is how I like my things to be. How can I change it?" As I explained earlier, every person has room for change. In this case, the first step to do is clean your house and organize your things. Maintain the habit of putting anything you use or displace back where it was. I know it is going to be hard for the first few weeks, but you can pass this test with flying colors if you're persistent and committed. As days go by and you grow accustomed to the tidiness of your place, you will realize how brighter and how comfortable your life will be.

Reward Progress. We have discussed that rewarding accomplishments conditions the mind into believing there's something to look forward to every time you make an effort. This is not only in the case of weight loss on the cheat day. It is also applicable if you plan to develop a useful habit towards Self-Transformation. Whenever you get something right, it is important to reward yourself. Buy anything you want. Eat anything you want. Or give yourself one day to just relax

Unstoppable Day

and do nothing. The cheat day is a necessity to keep discipline at its peak. Depriving the mind and the body of the things it wants does more harm than good. Trust me, starving the body of goodness slowly pulls the mind into discouragement, which may cause the total cessation of the process towards self-discipline and self-transformation. That is why it is important to give yourself a day off. It helps to forget about the stress, anxiety, and pressure your journey is putting upon you.

Chapter 4:
Surprising Mind Tricks to Master Self-Discipline

What is the secret of a magician? For starters, it is neither about the illusions nor the tricks up their sleeves. The real secret of a magician is the innocence of the naked eye. The reason why magicians never reveal their tricks is that when they do, it strips their illusions of their fun. Everybody would know how they do it. Nobody will be enticed to watch his show again.

I personally believe that everybody's a magician. They all have their way of doing things that other people cannot entirely understand. Some people have more self-discipline than others. Some took a shorter time to achieve Self-Transformation. Other people seem to make little effort to find success. What we don't realize is that there is a secret in everything these people do. To our innocent minds, it just seems to beat the impossible. It all seems like a magic show. Truth is, we don't know the extra efforts they put in their work. We don't know how they overcame their shortcomings. We have no idea how they acquired an unstoppable sense of self-discipline. As people with innocent eyes, we have no clue how they strived from the depths of their own hell. It is like watching Master Houdini escape from his chains of death.

Do not be discouraged if you feel like you have nothing to offer to the world. Each of us has a "magic" or skill that other people do not have. Every one of us has a forte that nobody else can beat. The trick to unleashing that power is by developing an amazing sense of self-discipline. Once you do, self-transformation will allow you to uncover your optimal potential to use it towards success. In this chapter, I will be showing you tricks to take control of your mind. These illusions will train the mind to unleash its full potential. As you see, these activities seem to be very common and easy to do, but what you do not know is it impacts the brain dramatically, training it to be better without even knowing. Are you ready to learn various magic techniques to trick your brain into self-discipline? Here are twelve mind tricks to get the most out of your brain.

Increase Intensity. If you have tried going to the gym, you might have noticed that once a person develops his resistance on a certain weight, he aims to add more intensity to his routine. Just like your brain, it needs an increasing amount of intensity to keep learning, to keep pushing, and to keep improving. If a person chooses to remain stagnant in his level of thinking, he will not make any improvement. Why does a person need to increase the threshold of his abilities? Simply put, as time passes by, challenges evolve along with it. As you push through the road to success, you will find your challenges harder each day. This is why you need to prepare yourself in various levels of adversity. It helps your mind adjust and cope easily, reducing your instances of breaking down.

Always look for an opportunity to grow. Do not be afraid to make mistakes because the lessons you learn from your experiences are timeless, and come in handy as you progress on each milestone. Do not be afraid to feel pain, once you've grown resistant to it, you will be stronger, bolder, and wiser every day.

Write it down. Did you know that writing your thoughts down can help you gain self-discipline? Unlike speaking, writing about your feelings can boost your concentration level and enhance your focusing skills. Pouring your feelings out using pen and paper not only grants mind control, but it can also help regulate a person's emotions. Psychologists have found that keeping a journal of your thoughts and feelings can help alleviate stress, sadness, and anxiety. Think of it as giving yourself a pep talk where you experience a lot of realizations and reflections to use later in life.

Keeping a journal is also effective in monitoring the progress of your self-transformation. You can write about how you feel about a task before, during, and after you accomplish it. This way, you will feel more motivated to keep pushing yourself into accomplishing more and more each day.

Unstoppable Day

Share your Goals. Sharing your goals with your friends and family has been proven to bring wonders to your journey towards success. Apart from the fact you can learn from their suggestions, they can also push you to your limit by motivating you into working hard. Family and friends can help uplift your spirit, especially in times of hardships. It will be best to know there are people who support and love you for who you are.

Sharing your goals with your loved ones is also a form of socialization. It allows you to interact, speak up, and assert yourself. It helps you rehearse how to deal with some of the timely crises in life. Furthermore, this can also help you adjust yourself in social situations. This may come in handy if you are shy. Your friends and family can help you develop your interpersonal skills.

Learn from your Mistakes. A lot of people out there get dissuaded every time they make a mistake. Always remember: we are only human. We are prone to making bad decisions. We are prone to wrong our fellowmen. You are born to make mistakes. Life wouldn't be called that way if it was easy. That is why we need to acknowledge that mistakes really are a part of our journey. Once we realize this, we will never hesitate to take another stepping stone. The fear of committing mistakes hinders us from being assertive. It depletes our confidence and commitment to our line of work. It fills our mind with self-doubt, which is detrimental to the progress of our Self-Transformation.

One of the most common reasons why a person is afraid to make mistakes is the reputation he upholds in society. He does not want to be ostracized by society. Be that as it may, it should not stop you from being yourself in doing what you need to achieve success. Your neighbors, no matter how perfect their life seems, commit mistakes too. Who knows? Maybe they made even worse mistakes than you. All you need to remember is that as long as your conscience remains clear and you know you're not stepping on others' toes, as long as you know that you are not violating any other people's rights, then you have nothing to worry about. Keep on doing what you need to, and society will come to accept the new you. Remember: you are not doing this for anyone else but yourself. For your own development.

There is no Right Time. Why wait when you can do it now? Lots of people are very hesitant to act courageously and take their first step towards success. The reason they keep buried in their minds is 'the right timing'. Ask yourself what is the root of that doubt pertaining to the "Right timing." If you are not going to do it now, when? Is it because you are not ready? Or is it because you are too lazy to think about it? Earlier, we came to the conclusion that time is the most precious commodity. Once it has passed, you can never take it back. The only thing that is getting between you and the right timing is your mindset. You don't control time to be ready for success. You control your mind to be willing to make an effort towards success. The problem is not the right timing. The problem is a strong mindset towards readiness and commitment to hard work.

Self-Motivation. What motivates you the most? Is it your dream, the people pushing you towards that dream, or both? If it's both, then consider yourself lucky. Some people out there strive towards success without the support from their loved ones. Some tread in the dark world all alone without any care or love from their family and friends. If you're one of those people who do not rely on anyone but themselves, this mind trick is for you. You don't have to rely on other people to feel motivated. You can motivate yourself. All it takes is a little bit of commitment, confidence, and self-discipline. Whenever you feel the need to give up or break down, stop for a moment and think. Signal your mind to stop thinking about the negativities that life brings you. Instead, focus on positive things. Put yourself in a calm and comfortable space, and think about what went right instead of what went wrong. Self-motivation is the key to moving forward without any glitches or self-doubt. If the world is giving you trouble and no one is there to support you, support yourself simply because you can. If you can motivate yourself on your own, you will find endless numbers of inspiration to focus on. Nothing will derail you on your way to success.

Say Thank You more often. Gratitude is a very important value among mankind. It fosters happiness, contentment, and simplicity in life. It avoids greed, avarice, and boastfulness that can make a person hit rock bottom. Saying thank you more often leads to a peaceful life.

Being thankful for what you have is better than pining over what you don't. It helps you avoid any temptation that makes you lose focus on your goals.

If it helps, you can include a list of people to thank in your journal. Write a short message about their regards, their help, even the small tokens of support. Thank the person who said you are pretty, handsome, or intelligent. Thank the person who handed you a cup of coffee at work. Smile at people in the streets. Help those people in need. That will make you realize there are good things in life to look forward to. It makes you believe that humanity still exists. If you are looking to change the world with your skills and talents, being grateful about the bounties that life can bring you is a vital step.

Never underestimate the allure of gratitude and thankfulness. It will provide you success along with happiness and contentment that will endure over time. Gratitude creates a legacy – something to remember you by even after your bones have turned to ashes.

Learn to Say Sorry. Apologizing for your mistakes is a major factor when aiming for a happy and contented lifestyle. It grants you the self-discipline to own up to your mistakes by sincerely asking for forgiveness. Having an apologetic mind can grant a life-long transformation and allows humility and modesty to blossom. These traits, laced with self-discipline, drive a person to success. By listening to the humble voice inside your head, it can bring wonders to your life.

Unstoppable Day

It allows you to learn from your mistakes and make up for what you did wrong.

Learn to Forgive. Forgiveness goes hand in hand with love. It does not have to be 'romantic' love, it could also mean love for your family, self, or line of work. Granting forgiveness to yourself and other people clears your mind and refreshes your soul. It promotes love, care, and support that adds to the motivation to strive harder in life. It allows us to keep moving forward and let go of the pain. Songs have been written and poems have been inscribed to show the value of forgiveness. However, it takes a lot of courage and self-discipline to forgive and forget the people who have wronged you. Once you have mastered the ability to understand and comprehend other people's mistakes, you will slowly regain control over your mind and emotions.

Learn to say No. There are a lot of temptations that will derail you on your road to self-discipline. As a mind trick, learn to say "No, thank you," especially when you know it can detract your focus on your goals. Just decline the offer and never look back. Saying "No" to specific activities can be hard at the beginning, more so if it is something you are used to. The trick into walking away from temptation is to believe that you are a completely different person. Think of it this way, there are two people trying to stop their addiction on alcohol. Person A was offered a twenty-percent discount from any merchandise in the liquor store but said, "I am sorry, I am trying to quit." Next, Person

B was offered the same, but he answered, "No, thank you. I am not that kind of person."

The difference between these two people is their self-perspective. Person A still believes he is addicted to alcohol, while Person B acknowledges that he has a different personality. Sometimes, our self-concept and our will to change can affect the difficulty of saying no to temptation. So, whenever you feel the need to get derailed, always remember you are not that person. You are a person who is on the road to self-discipline and there is nothing anyone can do to stop you.

Be Confident. It is effective to give yourself a pep talk from time to time. It grants you comfort and it guarantees everything is going to be okay. When you are faced with difficult adversity, create a good assurance to yourself that you can do it. Remind yourself of your skills and capabilities. Convince your mind that good things come out of being perseverant. Always remember, should you commit any mistakes, you can rise back up because you are strong enough to do so. Remind yourself of your inspirations, your family and friends. Tell yourself that they will always be there for you when you fall. You do not have to be afraid anymore.

Plan Good Things. In the journey to be a successful individual, it is important to be open to experience. If you have nothing else to do, plan a trip, go someplace else, try new things, or look for a new hobby.

Unstoppable Day

These are great ways to learn a lot from your experiences, something that might come in handy in the future. Planning good things is also an effective way to alleviate stress and reduce pressure, devastation, and anxiety. Consider it as a form of rest and recreation that also helps you learn and gain more knowledge about life.

You know what they say, "Life is not made to be lived in one place." If you travel to new places, you will meet new faces, experience different personalities, get immersed in different cultures, and learn life lessons. For instance, if you plan to travel around the globe, go to the places where Taoism and Buddhism are considered the main religion. In doing so, their elders will be able to teach you the secrets towards a happy life. They might even teach you more tricks to gain self-discipline and self-transformation through meditation. Experience what's like to live simply and peacefully. Let yourself gain realizations and reflections to apply when you come home. Open your mind to new knowledge and you will find yourself on the edge of becoming a master of your mind.

Chapter 5:
The Secrets to Resist Temptation

Acquiring well-established self-discipline is never easy, but neither impossible. To gain full control of the mind, you will need courage, commitment, and persistence to keep moving forward despite the numerous temptations that challenge your perception. Life will always throw you distractions that can detract your focus from your goals. Our goal is to cultivate resistance to your hardest temptations – to act in accordance with your thoughts, and not your impulses or feelings. The main challenge of acquiring well-rounded self-discipline is not how a person interprets a situation but how one controls one's emotional state.

For instance, an alcoholic person is trying to change his behavior. Whenever he is offered a drink, the problem is not how he interprets the temptation rather than how he feels about it. He might feel devastated because he misses the times when he used to get drunk and have fun with his friends. The memories of good times will cause frustration, now that he is being a "kill-joy" to his friends. When the body is desperate to relapse into old habits, a person becomes emotional about pursuing change. One temptation will lead to various reasons why you should sulk towards the dark side. Your mind will argue with you, saying, "This is not you. This does not feel right. Sooner or later, you will not have any friends left." If you let these thoughts intrude your progress towards success, you become a lost cause. These emotions that you emancipate trigger your sadness and desperation to go back to old times. They blur your focus on your long-term goals. These temptations blind you when it comes to self-transformation. Eventually, you will find yourself moping at point blank. These impulses and emotional tendencies should be controlled for unstoppable self-discipline.

I like to symbolize our self-discipline in the form of an iron fist. As we all know, the iron fist is a symbol imbued to people who have withstood the hardest of adversities. The iron fist is known for being steadfast, strong, and committed. It is a symbol of ruthless authority, which is what we need to resist our temptation. Think of it like being Superman, except you are surrounded by Kryptonite. To obtain the iron fist of self-discipline, you need to improve, cope, and adapt to resist opposing powers. Once a person's self-discipline is as strong as the iron fist, no temptation will shy him away from his goals. In this chapter, I will be discussing how to develop the iron fist of self-discipline. But first, let is tackle the types of temptation that can keep you from an unstoppable self-discipline

The Temptations of the Disciplined

The Temptation of The Past.

As you lay down at night, trying to get some sleep, your thoughts allow you to imagine things, remember moments, and go down memory lane. Some moments you remember are timeless, joyful memories that will always serve as an inspiration to your future. However, there are times when you feel the horror of your mistakes. Your mind reminisces the times you failed, the times you were embarrassed, the times you were fooled. The temptation of the past will drive your frustration to its peak, causing fear of another failure. It will make you paranoid about your current situation, afraid of anything that can or cannot happen, especially when you're trying to accomplish the goals you were not able to before.

The Temptation of The Future.

Another temptation that inhibits your ability to look past your mistakes is your anxiety of the future. It makes you fear the things you do because of their possible outcome. It makes you ask yourself different "What if's" that compromise your ability to think clearly and decide wisely on your challenges. Thinking about the future in a negative manner is a temptation that will make you hit rock bottom. It inhibits your ability to innovate, create, and grow as a person. It allows you to think about all of the setbacks and consequences your journey to transformation will cause. The temptation of the past, along with the temptation of the future, causes demotivation and stagnation in an individual. It hinders a person from keeping an eye on his goals, breaking his spirit of becoming a fully successful individual. Focusing on the past and future gives way to more than just frustration, as the deprivation of emotional self, torture, and depression are known to occur as well.

The Temptation of Procrastination.

One of the worst temptations that cause setbacks is procrastination. When your mind is filled with distractions and enticements, there's a huge probability you will give in. You will remember how amazing it is to finish a whole series of movies rather than doing something productive. You will see your old self; how simple your life was before you decided to venture towards Self-Transformation. Procrastination is a very powerful temptation that has caused lots of ships to burn down and crash in the ocean. It is likened to be a siren's song that distracts the minds of sailors in the middle of the ocean. For young minds, procrastination is the number one enemy towards success. There are literally hundreds of things to dissuade them from productiveness, such as gadgets, friends, gimmicks, and other activities.

The Temptation of Breaking Down

The problems you encounter in life will crush your spirit, pierce your soul and disengage your will to succeed. They will make you doubt your existence in the world, question who you are, your identity, and your belief in yourself. There are challenges that will ward off some friends and family who do not believe in you. But in those moments of loneliness, you will start to think twice about changing for the better.

Your mind will try to convince you things are getting worse. Success doesn't always mean money or fame. To millions of people out there, success means happiness and freedom from societal chains. To these people who aim for psychological and emotional success, breaking down is a common factor towards failure. You will think about how tired you are in this penitent. Your heart will start to feel heavy. It will feel like you're making all the wrong choices in life. Once you let the temptation of breaking down get into your soul, your mind and heart start to fall apart. It will clench your spirit and break your vital force. It frightens you take another step because you're afraid of pain, anguish, and frustration to move forward in your life. For me, this is the most difficult challenge to step out from.

The Temptation Between the Truth and The Lie.

In the previous chapter, we discussed integrity as one of the most vital keys to success. During your hardships on the road to self-transformation, you will be tempted to make immoral choices just to make your life easier. Sometimes, challenges force you to tell a lie and exaggerate the truth. These will soon spread into countless lies for the years to come. Once your body and mind start to believe the lies you have been telling people, your real identity is difficult to track. How can you transform yourself into something positive, when you don't know who you really are? You cannot achieve success if your life is built on deception. Eventually, these lies will catch up on to you, causing you a setback that can ruin your life for good. As much as possible, no matter how easy it is to lie, choose to speak –and believe in- the truth. Do not let yourself be consumed by the chain of lies you have created. Find out who you really are. Stand up to your beliefs. Nothing good ever happens to people who pretend to be someone they are not.

You have to admit; we all have been challenged by these temptations. If you remain where you are now, that means you have yielded your strength and gave in to any of these temptations. That's over now. Now that you know what you need to watch out for, here are the most important secrets to resist untimely temptations.

The Secrets Against Temptation

Focus on Your Identity.
Sticking with who you are is important to ward off the temptation between the truth and the lie. It allows you to be who you really are without any hint of treachery. When you focus on your identity, you start to live up to your strengths and acknowledge your weaknesses. You will start to discriminate opportunities from threats. Knowing who you are from the inside out will give you a higher-thinking ability to choose what is right, a trait only a few possess.

You do not have to pretend about anything. You are a unique individual who is way better in something than anybody else in the world. Learn to be satisfied with what you can give, and start to enrich it by learning and by practicing your skills. Pretentiousness causes unhappiness and dissatisfaction. It gives you unrealistic thoughts about your capabilities, increasing your self-expectation, even when you have reached your peak by being your true self. Though playing pretend can get you where you want very easily, soon thereafter, you will start to doubt everything in your life. You will start to realize the real you should be someplace else. *That* is where you should be, instead of pretending to be happy here. Start to live your life the way you want to, not the way others want you to. If you are afraid, they might not accept you, don't be. Your real friends and family will always be there for you no matter what you choose. As the saying goes, "Family is not always about blood. They are the people who care about and love you the most whoever you are." If they cannot accept you for what you can become, and it is not your loss. There will always be people who will accept you, especially on the road towards success and Self-Transformation.

Embrace Your Trigger

Throughout the course of our lives, we have encountered hardships, challenges, embarrassments, and failures, during which we have developed our own cues that trigger our emotionality. There are words, sights, and sounds that remind us of the negativities we have encountered before. Sometimes, these can bring motivation, and enhance our drive to work better and strive harder. However, often times they derail us from being productive for the day. Once these memories trigger sadness, it is very difficult to cope. It makes us idle and unproductive, sulking all day long, ruminating about the past when we should be focusing on the present. To prevent these emotional cues from ruining our day, we need to start embracing our emotional triggers.

The first step you take in healing from your trigger is to forgive yourself for your mistakes. To accept that you were young and knew nothing but to satiate your impulses. Acknowledge that people can change, and so can you. Times are different, you have grown for the better, and now you're trying to be a better person.

Next, you need to face your triggers with an iron fist. When you see something that reminds you of your past, take three deep breaths, and allow yourself to let go of the memory. It may cause pain and sadness, but when you accustom yourself to that feeling, it can no longer hurt you. Rather, it becomes a shield that makes you learn a lesson from your past. Forgive the people who have wronged you and reflect on what you did wrong as well. If it helps, write about it, express everything you never got to say before. Let it be a beacon for change and improvement in your life. Let it make you stronger and bolder to face more challenges in life.

The third step into healing from your emotional trigger is to detach yourself from the memory. Whenever you think of something bad about a situation, try to focus on something positive about it. If none, shift your focus on to something funny, attractive, or delicious. That way, your emotional trigger will not be able to hurt you anymore. Learn to relax your brain in the midst of being in pain, and do something that can ease your feelings about it rather than focusing on your negative feelings.

Embrace Discomfort

One of the things that inhibit a person from moving forward is the discomfort of pushing through. I am sure most of us have encountered the saying, "Get out of your comfort zone." No matter how much people speak about it, only a few have the guts to actually do it. Discomfort is a very advantageous form of learning. It makes you experience and overcome problems you have never dealt with before. Once you overcome these new issues and challenges, treading with different trials will be a walk in the park. To overcome temptations, you need to seek pain and get used to it. We have discussed earlier that the reason for temptation is not the interpretation of the mind, but feelings from the heart. If you get used to the pain and discomfort of doing something different, then you're one step closer towards Self-Transformation. Not only is discomfort a conduit for growth and development, but it also helps you overcome your fear of failure, anxiety, and depression. Embracing discomfort grants you the ability to be a Strong-Willed individual, in an unstoppable pursuit towards success.

Chapter 6:
Break the Cycle Holding You Back

The most dangerous phrase that holds a person back and results in repeated failure is "Just this once." Just this once, you want to eat chips because you have cravings. Just this once, you want to skip your exercise routine because you feel tired. Just this once, you want to sleep until 10 AM because you do not feel like waking up at five in the morning. Did you know that establishing a good habit takes a person many years to accomplish if he keeps on saying, "Just one more time?" Because of that "last" resort, a person reverts back to the old ways. Because of that one fall, he relapses back to where he came from and starts anew once again.

If you have come so far only to be tempted to roll back your old habits, you better think twice. Do you want your efforts to be worthwhile? Don't you want to have a groundbreaking change as you get older? Don't you want to do something productive in your life? If your answer is yes, you better not get into the temptation of reverting back to your old self.

In this chapter, I will be discussing the importance of positive habits and why bad habits inhibit your abilities to achieve success. First and foremost, what is a habit? A habit is a custom that is ingrained in your mind. All of your decisions and actions solely rely on those habits, like a primary nature. It governs how you act, talk, walk and even interact with people around you. Imagine having bad habits and how it puts you in a disadvantage.

If you have poor emotional and mental habits, you are inclined to be bossier, more insensitive, and greedy in your decisions. You have the predisposition to act on your impulses without thinking about the consequences of your actions. You choose poorly. You get upset over trifles. Imagine having an attitude like that. Do you really think you can achieve success with that kind of thinking?

For instance, you have bad behavioral habits such as being late, absent, and lazy. Top it up by being an alcoholic or a chain smoker. Where do you see yourself in five years?

As a person who's trying to change, there is always a way to break that cycle and create a new one. I believe that nobody's a lost cause. All you need to do is find a little bit of self-discipline in yourself, and all will work from there.

Habits are ingrained in our mind to satisfy short-term goals. If you have bad habits, then your actions will be against your own self-interest. They will cause you to fail over and over again, bringing you back to the depths of your own despair. However, if you have good habits, then your actions and decisions will be in accordance with your long-term goals. They will help you become whom you aspire to be and guide you where you need to be as years pass by.

Stages of A Habit
As we all know, understanding our weaknesses allows us to turn them into strengths. In this segment, we will be discussing the stages of a habit to find out exactly how to put up an intervention for our mind.

Cue
The cue signals the mind about the presence of a resource to do a habit. In weight loss, for example, the cu and e in this scenario are the chips and other unhealthy foods in the refrigerator. They entice the mind easily, given that they are just a few steps away, ready to be eaten.

Craving
The cue brings craving or the raging need to do the behavior. No matter how a part of the mind tries to dissuade the body from doing it, craving takes over and convinces the body to do otherwise.

Routine
When the mind and body have already been convinced that it is okay to give in to the temptation, a person is inclined to do the behavior. The routine stage is also known as compulsive behavior. This is the stage for a person acts on his impulses without thinking.

Reward

This is the ultimate reason a habit is performed over and over again. When the craving has been satiated, the body feels relief, and the mind feels happiness and satisfaction. When the behavior is rewarded, there's a bigger chance the person will do it again.

Break the Routine

Thought-Stopping

Whenever intrusive thoughts take control of the mind, practice thought-stopping. The causes of this concept help a person develop well-rounded self-discipline towards Self-Transformation. Thought-stopping means to literally stop thinking negative thoughts and redirecting them into something else. This is a cognitive intervention, usually prescribed by psychologists and psychiatrists to interrupt the intrusive thoughts of the depressed and anxious. This works extremely well too in eliminating an obsession, urge, and bad, unwanted habits.

Psychologists believe that in order to perform thought-stopping, you need to consider three simple steps:

- Focus on the present. What are your goals? Where do you see yourself in a year or two? What would it mean for you that your intrusive thoughts hinder you from pursuing your dreams?

- Give yourself a pep talk. Dissuade yourself whenever wanting to do that habit again. What are the disadvantages? How does it affect you personally? How does it affect your goals? Do you really want to be that person again? As much as possible, keep your mind off of the temptation.

- Keep a journal. Whenever something bothers your mind, make sure you keep a journal with you and start writing about it. Writing your thoughts and emotions down can help you think rationally despite the intrusive thoughts. It allows you to decide clearly on what is needed to overcome each temptation that comes into your mind.

- To furnish your ability in thought-stopping, you need to learn how to relax your mind through breathing and reciting a mantra. Clear your head. Recite a chosen mantra ten times while breathing deeply. Do this whenever you feel tempted to resort back to old habits, as it can help you keep your mind off of things, especially the temptations life can bring.

Visualization.
A lot of people remain skeptic about the value of visualization, but what people don't know is that you can turn these images into a reality. The mental picture that flows in your mind becomes imbued with your heart. Thinking about it comforts you. Your goals make you feel like home. So, whenever you feel tempted in any way, once you

visualize your goals, it would feel like every trial would just fade away. The feeling of your thoughts running through your veins will be like a 'refresh' that clears your head of the things you need to do and what you need to become. When you visualize your future, you will feel a sudden relief. It will make you realize there is something to look up to. There is a reward for every effort, and all of your hardships mean something to your life.

The visualization of your dreams and aspirations increases your performance at its peak. It makes you believe in yourself, gain confidence and determination to pursue another day without fear. It makes you more innovative and creative, unafraid to generate new ideas towards success. The visualization of your future brings motivation to do -and the self-discipline to avoid- behaviors. Other people think visualization is an old wives' tale told to children to push them to their limits. What they don't is that if you really perform this concept, it can bring wonders to your life you can't even fathom.

Think of A Reason

To break the cycle of your bad habits, you need to think of a reason why you should stop. Whether it is about your health, your physical appearance, your career, even your loved ones, create a reason to dissuade you from ever performing a bad habit again. For example, if your goal is to lose weight, ask yourself, why do you need to lose weight in the first place? List all of the reasons why you want to achieve a beach body: Whom do you want to impress? What do you want to accomplish? What do you want to see in the mirror?

Remind yourself that you are tired of all the bullying and teasing. Remind yourself of the inconvenience of having all that extra weight. How you were not able to climb the peak of the mountain because of your lack of stamina and shortness of breath. How your clothes will not fit you anymore and you need to buy lots of new ones to fill an empty cabinet. Think all of these reasons as a form of improvement and motivation. Let these hardships be a persuasion for you to work harder and never resort to your old ways. Do not take this as a demotivation for not being good enough. Rather, take it as a challenge and convince yourself that you can do it. Other people could. Some reported to having lost 98 pounds in 21 days. Others said they lost more. Now that you have this book, you are more empowered to work hard, especially now that you know the secrets towards unstoppable self-discipline.

Find A Replacement, Workout, Or Sports

As discussed earlier, the main reason why a habit is repeated over and over again is the reward. The most common way to avoid the temptation towards a relapse is to find a replacement with the same effect or parallel to the effect of the bad habit. For example, if your habit is smoking or binge-drinking alcohol, you might want to consider trying new hobbies such as working out or doing sports. These two can also help elicit the satisfaction you get from smoking cigars and drinking alcohol. Workout, along with sports, helps the body release sufficient amounts of endorphins –feel-good hormones- to feel happy and energetic throughout the day.

In your weight loss challenge, if your problem is your craving for oily foods and chips, you can try replacing these with fruits and vegetables. If you're not accustomed to this behavior, it might seem very odd and discomforting at first, but trust me, once your body has endured enough to resist the temptation towards junk foods, it means you have released yourself from the chains of your bad habits.

Another key to making this concept work is restricting all access to bad habits. Remember, out of sight, out of mind. If there is nothing accessible to cue temptation, then the mind is not inclined to crave for that habit ever again.

Share your Goal

Did you know that sharing your goals and principles with your family members and friends can help you stick to your goals? Having people around to support you actually feels good, especially when you are trying to accomplish difficult goals. They will be there to uplift your spirit in your times of hardships. Share your goals with them and they can help you ward off any temptation that comes into your way. Your family and friends will make sure you get the transformation you need by pushing you forward and motivating you to stick to your vision. The best part of sharing your goal is the learning you gain from interacting with your loved ones. Your parents will always have suggestions to help you maintain a good sense of self-discipline towards success. Your friends probably have other experiences regarding your problems. They, too, can help you maintain a stable mindset.

Challenge Yourself

The extinction of your bad habits may consist of the balance between reward and punishment. Have you ever heard of classical conditioning, developed by Ivan Pavlov? If not, well this is a chance to furnish your self-discipline using a bit of psychological practice. See, Ivan Pavlov discovered that a behavior paired with reward is more likely to be repeated. However, if a behavior is paired with punishment, then the habit is more likely to diminish.

Much like the development of self-discipline, you need to learn when to reward and punish yourself. Challenge yourself for one week to abstain from your old habits. Create a timeline for each day and track your improvements. For every day that you do not do the bad behavior, you reward yourself with something you like (but not a bad habit, obviously). However, if you find yourself violating your promise and feeling on your goals for the day, create your own punishment and stick to it. If you like, you can have some family members and friends help you track your improvements and initiate your reward and punishment system. For example, every time that you commit a bad habit, you will be forced to put $10 or $20.00 in a jar. Or, you will be forced to give up TV privileges. Maybe even dinner.

Brendon T. Walker

I remember a few years ago, I had a friend who used to swear all the time. When he wanted to change, I had the idea of making a swear jar. So, whenever he spoke a bad word, he would be forced to put $10.00 into the jar, and he would never get it back. We would spend the money without him and send him pictures of how we used his swear jar money. This pushed him to stop talking whenever he had the urge to swear or say a bad word about someone. Now, he is a motivational speaker to teenagers about suicide and depression. Amazing how self-disciplined works for committed individuals!

Chapter 7:
Getting Work Done Even if You're Lazy

Do you ever have those days when you wake up the morning and want to do nothing except lie down and watch television all day? Do you ever get that feeling of being lost? These days where you have billions of thoughts in your mind but no energy to do anything. It is the feeling of emptiness and discouragement that inhibits your ability to think and be productive for the day. You feel completely numb, not even thinking about the consequences of unproductivity. It is like you could not care less about your future anymore.

Procrastination makes easy things hard, hard things harder.

Mason Cooley

Laziness is characterized by idleness and stagnation. It is the most dangerous habit to develop, especially for someone who aspires to succeed. If you're starting to feel like you need to procrastinate, you better rethink your choices and never give into it. As we have discussed earlier, the reason for obtaining a habit is the reward you get from the behavior. When you procrastinate, you get rewarded for the happiness and joy you feel from watching the TV all day long, or through surfing the Internet. You are inclined to resort to a diet that is detrimental to your health. What's worse, when you procrastinate, there's a tendency that your mind becomes hyperactive in a negative way. It reminds you every mistake you have ever made, of who you were before. It guilts you into becoming a fully-transformed individual.

A lot of people think that laziness is just that – unproductiveness. That there is a reason behind a person's resort to procrastination. In light of this, here are five reasons why a person gives in to the temptation of procrastination.

Demotivation

When a person loses an inspiration to reach for the stars, he becomes idle and unproductive. He thinks, "Why would I be doing this if I can have fun instead?" This usually happens when great adversity strips a dreamer from his soul, like the death of a loved one, a broken heart, or a failed plan. Demotivation occurs when a person forgets who he is and whom he wants to be. Knowing the hardships in life, it will provide various challenges that could test the mindset of an individual. These trials can come in the form of untimely advice to test one's beliefs. It can come from calamities or so-called "signs." Sometimes, people ostracize and disregard something they don't understand, instead of trying to keep up with it. They treat it like garbage. On the road to Self-Transformation, lots of people will tell you how they loved you for who you were before you decided to change. There are people who can dissuade you by providing enticing points such as missing the gimmicks and other happy memories. Some will tell you that you are still pretty young to be doing all those things and that you should be enjoying your life while it lasts, not go rushing yourself to be mature.

But ask yourself whom you want to be in the future, not whom they want you to be right now. Ask yourself: do you want to invest your time doing nothing? Or do you want to be productive, to have long-lasting happiness in the near future? See, there is advice that you should listen to, especially if it is about lifting yourself, changing for the better, and solving your problems. However, there is also advice you should never listen to, especially when it holds you back. The decision is entirely up to you. Only you can live your life, nobody else.

Weariness

When a person starts to lose energy, persistence goes away too. Weariness can influence a person to become unproductive and lazy. It argues with the mind about how the body needs rest, even when it doesn't. It reminds the heart about the difficult trials it has overcome and says it needs some rest to recover, even when you have had enough time to lay low. Don't get me wrong, resting the mind and body is a vital process that allows rejuvenation and alleviation of stress, but sometimes, when the mind becomes greedy of its rewards, it pushes the body to procrastinate.

Emotionality

Some people are highly sensitive to their emotions. They easily get triggered through words, objects, smells, or people. Being emotional can hinder you from reaching your peak. It clouds your mind in the midst of adversity. The mind is a very powerful tool; it can control the heart and the body. It is true that sadness and anxiety have physiological effects. They make a person physically weak, unproductive, and idle. The moment you let your mind think you are sad or anxious about something, you will be unable to perform your duties and your routines well. Nothing will interest you, and your daily routine will cease. You will not be able to work out, eat, sleep, and focus. All of which can have a huge negative impact on your goals.

Fear of Failure

When a person is afraid of trying, he resorts to procrastination. When he overthinks the future in a negative way, he will be demotivated to try harder. The fear of failure, much like the temptation of the future, is one of the hardest challenges to overcome, especially to people who have a flying imagination and an anxious mind. If you keep thinking about the future in a negative manner, it will be like putting your life in a pit you built yourself. It will start to devour your aspirations and dreams, along with your short-term goals. The fear of failure is a very dangerous tread. It makes you imagine things that aren't there, think of situations that can never happen, doubt the totality of your capabilities and it slowly depletes your confidence as a creative human being.

Inattentiveness to Goals

Losing sight of your goal can put you in the pit of procrastination. As the tunnel gets darker, it becomes harder for you to keep track of your dreams. Everything becomes a blur and you suddenly forget the reasons for striving hard. Being inattentive to your goal means that you neglect to remind yourself of whom you want to be. It degrades your persistence and determination to fight for what you believe in. A lost vision is more dangerous than any other temptation. You lose your purpose; you forget your viewpoint and you resort back to old ways.

Stay Away from The Black Hole

Procrastination is like a big black hole. It sucks all life and light it gets in contact with. If you are slowly feeling the emptiness and you want to just sulk in the couch to "enjoy" or "rest," you have come this far to even think about giving in. Once you let yourself get buried in that black hole, it becomes difficult to rise back up.

Procrastination is the art of keeping up with yesterday.

Don Marquis

Indeed, when you let yourself get sucked by its gravity, it will be like resorting to whom you were before rather than putting an effort to build your future self. As an emergency protocol, you need to remember these 10 simple steps to get you out of that couch and avoid the streaming gravity towards laziness.

Think of The Benefits

Before you sit in that couch and turn on the television, stop to think about why you need to accomplish your objectives for the day. Is there a potential income? Do they help you lose weight? Will they make you a better person? If so, you have plenty of reasons to avoid procrastination. Thinking of the benefits can make you focus on your goals and be reminded of your long-term desires.

Think of The Consequences

As you think of the benefits, think about the consequences if you aren't able to meet the deadlines. What do you think will happen if you do not finish your requirements on time? Think about the demerits, the challenges, the penalties. This will not only push you to move, but it also pushes you to work harder.

Visualize

Set your mind on your vision. Look for the piece of paper where you have written and drawn your dreams and aspirations for the future. Remind yourself why you started walking this road in the first place. Remember your dreams. What do you want to do for yourself? Your family? Your career? Your relationship?

Learn to Rest

Taking a break is a very important source of energy and motivation. As we have discussed earlier, laziness is caused by restlessness. On the road to success and Self-Transformation, you need to find a balance between procrastination and respite. If possible, create a schedule for your break time. That way, you can avoid getting in the brink of laziness and be on your way to productiveness.

Do Things One at A Time

In a day, there are various activities to accomplish. Thinking about these objectives can cramp out the brain, which is why you need to create a schedule of your daily tasks so you can do them one by one. Remember to rest for a reasonable number of minutes in between tasks to avoid mental and physical fatigue.

Break Down Tasks

To break down tasks, you need to organize and group your tasks into categories. Manage your tasks done at home, school, and work separately. From these variations, further group the objectives from easiest to the most difficult to accomplish and start from there. Whenever you go to school, take the checklist with you and try to accomplish what you can. Do the same when you get to work and when you go home.

Commit to A Schedule

Once you have created the schedule, you need to push yourself to follow what you have planned. On the road to self-discipline, you need to learn to commit even to the most basic plans. In the beginning, committing and persisting to accomplish your goals is difficult, but once your body is accustomed to it, you will be doing your tasks without even thinking about your schedule. Think about this as 'training' for your future endeavors in school, work, and family. If your attitude remains stagnant, you will never learn to adjust and cope with more difficult adversities. As small and simple as your plans may be, committing to them is a stepping stone towards a more productive and successful life.

Eat Healthily

Eating nutritious food can balance your hormones and chemical structure. It provides 'feel-good' and 'satisfaction' hormones that can help you become more motivated and hard-working, whereas eating junk food and oily foods make the brain sluggish and the body weary. When you eat fruits and vegetables instead of chips and fries, your productivity can increase dramatically and your decision-making and problem-solving abilities are enhanced greatly.

Sleep Well

Getting enough sleep is a way to rejuvenate your body after a long day's work. It helps the mind recharge and reorganizes its contents, leaving it fully refreshed and ready to face the troubles of a new day. Sleep is the stage where the body revitalizes holistically; it resets the effects of stress and hormonal imbalance, reestablishing homeostasis in our physical, mental, and emotional well-being.

Work Out Regularly

Working out regularly can increase the production of endorphins. It decreases the onset of sadness and anxiety, which is why it diminishes a person's chances of feeling emotional. The feel-good hormone prevents overthinking, avoiding stress and mental fatigue. It helps save more energy to be used on more important aspects of life such as working or studying. Instead of moping in bed or on the couch, it is vital to start moving and do some stretching to avoid getting stuck in the gravity of procrastination.

I am sure you can think of other ways to overcome procrastination. However, if you do not stick to your commitment to yourself, every effort you ever elicit towards your goals will be in vain. Instead of looking back down from where you left off, focus on the journey ahead. You have come so far only to let yourself get pulled back once again. Procrastination is yet another challenge. Think about its temporariness: when you start to forget about it, it will gradually disappear from your sight. Your choices are one hundred percent yours. You can either choose to get stuck in the black hole, or you can choose to walk the path of light.

Chapter 8:
Why You Need a Long-Term Morning Routine

"Morning is an important time of day, because how you spend your morning can often tell you what kind of day you are going to have."

Lemony Snicker

Most people disregard the value of mornings as their way of procrastination. Every time we wake up, we feel very frustrated saying, "Ugh, it's morning again!" We have this urge to press the snooze button and go straight back to sleep, thinking that it is okay to miss breakfast before you go to work or school. Instead of waking up at around five or six in the morning to accomplish more daily tasks, we prefer to wake up at seven saying, "I can do it all before ten."

Admit it; it took you years before you discovered the value of rising early. When you were younger, it was possible to delay work and stay up late and skip school. Because it felt better to sleep everything off. It felt like your worries fade away instantly.

But now that you have reached the point in life where you should actually persevere, those late morning habits are difficult to shake away. Now that you have bigger responsibilities, it's time to ban yourself from the snooze button and get yourself an effective morning routine.

Did you know that the most successful people wake up as early as 3:00 AM just to finish their morning routines, and be ready for work? Morning routine plays a role in the definition of a person's success. Not only does it help an individual be more productive, but the morning routine is also another milestone towards self-discipline. Just by not hitting the snooze button, you can feel a lot of improvement in your mindset and your body clock.

Morning is the most important time of day. It defines how you face the problems and trials of your day. It predicts the outcome of your activities, and it plans the schedule of your body and mind. Early mornings allow you to gather your composure before you start with a new day. They inhibit the chance of rushing towards your activities.

Imagine you wake up late. You have no time to cook and eat breakfast. Therefore, you are inclined to eat unhealthy foods from fast-food chains. You have no time to clean and prep yourself properly, which can decrease your confidence when dealing with people. What's worse, with all the cramming and traffic, you will be haggard by the time you get to work.

Setting the tone of your mind and body is a vital key to a successful day. It puts you in a mood that can lessen your frustration, anxiety, and emotionality. This may come as a shock, but early morning routines can make you stronger, holistically speaking. They alleviate stress levels, maintain bodily homeostasis, and improve your overall habit. The question is, "Where do I start?"

Luckily, I have concocted a list of an amazing early morning schedule that can tune you up, ready for anything. First, set your alarm to wake up early. About 4 or 5 AM would be nice. If you can do it at 3 AM, have a go. Once your alarm sets off, get up as fast as you can and never look back on your watch or your bed. Snoozing the alarm breaks your momentum off to start the day on the right foot. By giving in to this temptation, it will be like accepting your failure and resorting back to laziness. Have a little self-discipline and work your way up from there. Avoid telling yourself, "five more minutes" because it is the most dangerous phrase of all time. From there, you can do these eight routines every morning for a week or two, and you can even improvise.

- Go to the Mirror and Smile at yourself. You might think this is silly but it promotes positivity to flow into your body and mind. Smiling at yourself without any apparent reason for at least 15 seconds allows you to have some charisma that attracts positivity in your day. After doing this, you can observe the difference when you deal with people. You will start to be happier and more approachable towards those around you.

Unstoppable Day

- This day is different. While you are at it, remind yourself that today is another day and it is going to be legendary. Recap what you want to accomplish for this day. Who do you want to be at the end of the day? What do you want to learn? What kind of people do you want to meet? By setting these early goals, you can visualize and attract opportunities to come your way. Plus, it aids courage and strength to face the challenges of a new beginning.

- Make your Bed. Making your bed is the first physical exercise you should do every morning. Not only does it kick-start your blood flowing, but it also marks the first accomplishment of your day. By making your bed, you are acknowledging productiveness instead of procrastination. An activity as simple as that can signal your mind that you are more than a person who dreams. You are a person who is willing to make those dreams a reality.

- Clean a little. A little vacuuming or dusting in the morning is important. If you can do some laundry, then you have accomplished another goal. Cleaning gets rid of idle time. It detracts your focus from laziness and it pushes the body to keep moving forward.

- Meditate. To some, meditation is a mouthful, and a very difficult activity to accomplish. However, you do not need a yoga mat, or to pose like an Indian to meditate. You can just sit on your chair or sit on the bed while you relax your mind. Concentrate your vision into something beautiful, like your dreams. By meditating, you are relaxing your body and mind by focusing it into a safe and happy place. It enhances your motivation and persistence to go forth the day and accomplish your tasks with flying colors.

- Meditation facilitates mindfulness or awareness of the self and the environment. By meditating, you can assess your feelings and your thoughts. So, whenever something negative pops up, you will be ready to give yourself a pep talk or a motivational speech.

- Write a Gratitude Journal.

I love that this morning's sunrise does not define itself by last night's sunset.

Steve Maraboli

Gratitude fosters positivity in so many ways. It emphasizes your skills and lessens your self-doubt. It makes room for self-support and self-regard, increasing confidence and determination to succeed. By keeping a gratitude journal and writing on it every morning, you are reminded of your accomplishments instead of your failures. It reminds you of what you have rather than what you do not. It makes you thankful for a new day, a new chance to live. It makes you value your time and not waste any single moment.

When writing on your gratitude journal, bask on the blessings that life has offered you. Thank your parents for their love, your friends for their support, even the vendor who sold you coffee yesterday and gave you extra sugar. Appreciating these little things makes you a renowned and transformed individual.

Work Out

Even if you are not aiming to lose weight, it is still essential to work out and sweat a little. We have discussed that exercise helps the body release endorphins and maintain homeostasis. To obtain that warm and happy feeling before you go to work or school, make time to work out for even just half an hour.

Prepare A Nutritious Meal and Prep Yourself

Once you've accomplished these tasks, it is time to prepare the most important meal of the day – breakfast. To avoid stopping at fast food chains to eat some oily and unhealthy meal, why not prepare breakfast on your own? This way, you can control your calories intake and focus on your meal to avoid overeating. At home, you can eat fruits and vegetables, cereals, even enjoy that cup of tea without rushing and bumping into people. For this, you can listen to music or watch the early morning news to stay updated. In any case, watch out for your time or you might be late.

After eating breakfast, take time to prepare yourself to feel good about your appearance and gain confidence while interacting. Having an early morning routine allows you to choose your outfit carefully, and prepare without any glitch, rush, or panic. Then, you can finally leave home and be more determined than ever. You can start fresh at work, and stay calm as you face different adversities or stressors.

"I get up every morning and it's going to be a great day. You never know when it's going to be over so I refuse to have a bad day."

Paul Henderson

Self-Awareness
Wherever you go, whether it is school or work, always remember to keep a good character and own it. Even if it feels wrong or uncomfortable at times to change your attitude and traits, to build a strong sense of control, you need to take a good grip on your impulses and predispositions. Maintaining a great attitude towards your activities helps you boost your self-esteem because it allows you to foster self-awareness. The better a person knows himself, the more inclined he is to know his area of expertise. Apart from that, a person starts to understand himself more – his compulsion, temperament, and tendencies. Every detail he denies and represses becomes a part of his personality. Instead of disregarding his shadow or dark side, he starts to welcome it and train it towards something good.

I would like to share a short story about my cousin who was a bully in high school. See, he had a strong physique. He had a large body and stature. All my life, I have lived with him and watched as he made

Unstoppable Day

smaller boys cry in the classroom, and in the streets. Sometimes, he even makes our younger cousins cry, including me. When I was a kid, I was very thin and weak. He would always boss me around, toss me wherever and whenever he wanted it. Every time we play with him, he wanted to be superior. My cousin Bob would do everything to win. Of course, at the time, we only knew him as a bully, feared by most of our neighbors and playmates. We did not care to dig deep about the hidden reason. See, me and Bob were at the same age. But to my luck, we never became classmates until senior year. During this age, you would expect people to be more mature. But my cousin never changed a thing. He still bullied people in and out of school, had detention, and got suspended from time to time.

One Saturday afternoon, me and my mom happened to pay them a visit at their home. We were neighbors, so it was convenient to go from one house to the other. I was surprised to see him buried in his books, crying in the living room. But when he saw us enter, he quickly dried his eyes, gave me a sharp look and went to his bedroom. My mother asked why he was sobbing and Bob's mom said that he punished him for not doing good enough in Math.

I felt a pact of pity in my stomach but I did not show it to them. I walked towards his room and asked him to open the door. At first, he was hesitant. He threatened me that he will break my arm if I try to open his door. I said, "Okay, then I will wait for you here." After how many minutes, he came out because he had to pee. That was my shot of initiating a small talk.

It was awkward at first. Bob and I never really clicked. But I would bother me at night if I did not ask him. Only to find out that his mother brutally punishes him whenever he does not get a minimum of a B. We all have to admit that Bob is not much in academics. But he was good in martial arts. As he spoke, I realized that he was not aware of his actions toward other people. Bob opened the number of times he has asked for our classmates to tutor him but everyone declined. He felt like he had nobody and he felt like he is nothing.

It was my chance to tell Bob how he has been for almost 6 years. It turns out, he did not mean to push people around like that. He just wanted to gain some friends by being funny. He did not know he was being mean. Maybe it was his outlet of all the pain his mom had inflicted on him. Maybe it was a reflection of what he feels inside. Since that day, Bob tried to change his attitude and characteristics in school. Whenever he has the urge to bully or be mean to someone, he goes to the gym and play sports. After how many months of practice, we were surprised to see him as a different person. Bob started to enroll in Mixed Martial Arts and competed throughout the state for medals and trophies.

See, no matter how difficult for people to change, it is not hopeless. It always starts with self-awareness. In the morning when you wake

Unstoppable Day

up, try to get to know yourself better and better each day. Monitor your mood swings, your behavior towards that mood swings. And whenever you feel like having a fit, divert it into something productive instead.

Every morning when you walk or transport to school or work, close your eyes for a moment and think, "Who am I? What am I capable of?" Start to focus on everything around you – the air, your breathing, the sounds, your thoughts. Start to analyze how you feel about it. Get to know the hidden traits of your persona. Do not be afraid of taking the dark side along with the good. To foster a positive attitude towards life, you're going to need all the self-discipline you need to focus that negative energy into something you can be good at. If you are sad, try to write a poem or a song about it. Draw or paint your feelings out as if you are pouring your heart out through art. If you are an angry and irritable person, join the gym, engage in football, mixed martial arts or other sports. Wherever your heart leads you, as long as you let your mind control your impulses, you will discover your unspeakable strength towards your success.

Chapter 9:
How to Multiply Your Time

You might wonder sometimes, "How the hell do people accomplish so many things in just 8 hours?" In that time, only a few can really make something productive. The rest sulk into procrastination.

The secret towards accomplishment is not how you manage your time. It is how you manage yourself. In the first chapters, we discussed the value of self-management in relation to achieving success. In this segment, we will be discussing more about self-management and how to practice it in the long run.

There is actually no way to control time. Every minute will run whether you like it or not. The reason for unproductiveness is not because of how one schedules his time, it is how one conditions the mind and body.

For example, you have a lot of requirements due the next day. On your daily schedule, you have set 8:00 AM to 12:00 noon to do your assignments. You know that 4 hours is more than enough to get things done, but by the clock stroke twelve, you only finished about half. So, what could be the reasons why you were not able to accomplish your tasks?

This time, it was not because of the temptation of procrastination. You know, deep down, that you sat down in front of the computer for the whole 4 hours. You also know that it was not your emotionality because you kept your focus into doing your job. So, how come you did not finish it, even when you know you could have?

The main reason for this is not giving your mind and body what they need. Our thinking minds have their own mood swings too, believe it or not. They define the rate of progress we do in each activity. When a person is unable to condition his mind to think for that particular activity, he is more likely to be unproductive. It will be like your brain is not in the mood to think. Therefore, it slows down your progress, keeping you from finishing your requirements on time.

Much like our emotions, there are also tricks that we could use to fool the mind into doing tasks, even if it is not in the "mood." Let's face it, our minds could suddenly lie low, especially in situations when we really need to think the most. This is what people usually call 'blank-minded' or unable to think perhaps because of information overload, weariness, or stress. But not to worry, in this chapter, we will discuss how you can manage your mind to drive your body towards productiveness and avoid idle time.

Get Your Mind in The Mood

Know your Priorities. First and foremost, you must know your priorities well. Learn to organize your tasks from the most to the least urgent. Overthinking can cause anxiety and stress to an individual, causing the mind to perform according to one's problems and not one's goals. This keeps us from focusing and thinking clearly.

To aid you in this trick, gather a pen and paper and organize the deadlines of your requirements. What do you need to submit later? Tomorrow? The next day? You need to start tracking. Whether or not it is difficult to accomplish, the real key is not its hardship. Rather, your focus is the one driving your mind to finish the impossible. As you work through your list, check the ones you have finished and move on to the next. Remember to take a good rest before you begin another task, you would not want to strain your brain into fatigue. If you do, you will not be able to perform well.

Learn to Say No. There are times when we are asked to do something or go somewhere with someone. Often, we feel guilty to say no. For this, we need to rethink our priorities and start saying "no" comfortably. Also, when you decline offers and gimmicks, you must request a raincheck politely and make them understand why.

There are also instances in which we are offered a lot of opportunities. Although these are not bad at all, we need to learn how to evaluate our tasks. Yes, it can be flattering to be asked on a job interview or to speak in a seminar, but on your busy schedule, think of what you

Unstoppable Day

can accomplish if you say yes to every opportunity that comes knocking on your door. Even if you say you can do it, imagine how it can impact your physical and psychological health.

Stay off the internet and the TV. Unless you are using them for research, you better keep your gadgets turned off for your own good. Have you ever experienced spending hours on Facebook, even if you said it wouldn't be longer than 15 minutes? Social media does that to you. It makes you lose track of time. It entices you to stay for another minute until it becomes 60 more. To prevent any more distractions, turn off your phone, and put it someplace you cannot see it.

Turn your Messenger off. Actually, turn all your messaging apps off. When a friend or a loved one calls, it is very difficult to put down the phone, especially when you are talking about something funny or serious. Deactivate your messenger for a while until you finish what you need for your requirements. The calls and texts you receive can impede your momentum of thoughts in working or doing assignments. It makes you forget the next concepts to write about and the next activities to finish off. So, if you want to stay productive and maximize your time, have your

"me" time away from any temptations. Also, these tricks will allow the mind to focus on more important goals rather than surfing the web or watching a movie. Those memes will be there after you finish. You can re-watch the movies on Netflix anytime you want. You need to solve your problems first.

Post your schedule on a wall. When you are at home, there are a lot of enticements to overcome. Looking at the couch and the bed is one of the worst distractions. So, if you are tempted to sit and turn on the TV, put a schedule near the couch or near the TV. That way, you can guilt yourself into becoming more productive. Reminding yourself over and over about the goals will motivate you to finish all your tasks. At the same time, when you see the checkmarks on your goal, you will soon take pride in your actions. And you will thank yourself for that schedule on the wall.

Put some motivational quotes on a wall. If this sounds corny for you, why not write some messages on the walls. Whenever you want to eat junk food, put a message on the refrigerator that says, "You are going remain a big fat loser if you keep defeating yourself with that habit." Or when you want to watch TV instead, you can put a sticky note that says "Nothing good ever happens when you watch TV. Anyway, there are no good shows to see yet." These messages, although small, can help you lift your hopes up into focusing on what you need to do.

The Death Bed Dilemma. Whenever you doubt whether or not to do those tasks, imagine yourself on your death bed. "Will I regret not doing this for the rest of my life? What if this is the breakthrough that I have been waiting for?" This question works almost every time,

Unstoppable Day

especially on important tasks or duties. People think about not doing tons of things and they feel guilty because of the question "What if?" It is better to accomplish things and seize opportunities as they come. If you don't, you will be left asking yourself the most difficult question in the whole world. If you do not at least try, your life will start to be full of regrets. You will never know if that opportunity would have given you the success you deserved.

Wake up earlier. When you need to accomplish more goals, avoid staying up late. It makes the brain wobbly in the morning. Instead, try sleeping early when you are tired and wake up earlier the next day. This will kick-start your energy while you focus on your goals. Plus, it helps you think clearly about your requirements.

Chapter 10:
The Science Behind Why You Procrastinate

In previous chapters, we briefly discussed the main reasons behind a person's procrastination. Who knew that procrastination has an even deeper science of procrastination? In this chapter, I will be discussing the most notorious roots of procrastination that influences people all around the world.

If you feel like everything is hopeless because of your inability to focus on your goals, look around, everybody experiences it as much as you do. The unlucky few have it even harder. See, procrastination has something to do with one's life logic. It is caused by the imbalance of thoughts in your mind that inhibits your ability to feel good about doing things, and actually doing it. It is the manner of convincing yourself where and when you are going to do it without using the word "Later" or "Tomorrow."

These words, among many other phrases such as, "I am not in the mood," are very harmful to achieving your short-term and long-term goals. In life, there are literally millions of heartbreaking and mood-altering reasons not to put effort at all. Today, you are not in a good mood because you are tired of your past activities. Who is to say you will be in a good mood tomorrow morning? What if there is adversity that makes you feel demotivated once again?

These factors must not be tolerated to ensure your productivity as a person. As you work through this list of reasons why people procrastinate, you will see that the power of your mind is the most important tool to get out of this black hole.

Tiredness

Whenever a person feels restless in doing his everyday routine, he tends to lose focus on his long-term goals. Therefore, he procrastinates even more. But this is not the only reason why a person gets stuck in the black hole. Whenever an individual feels tired of everything he is experiencing at the moment, he tends to be demotivated to push through with his goals. There are many factors that contribute to one's tiredness: pain, anguish, and suffering from other aspects of life such as relationships, friendships, or family. Sometimes a person gets tired of putting up with every problem he has, which is why he starts to lose sight of his dreams or long-term goals.

There is no harm in resting from time to time because it adds energy to one's willpower. However, too much rest can cause idleness and stagnation bordering on unproductiveness. There's also no harm in detracting from time to time to solve problems unrelated to one's long-term goals. To focus better on the road towards success, it is essential to break down the building blocks that cause loss of progress.

Anxiety

Anxiety and apprehension regarding the future. People with anxiety usually think negatively about the future. They overthink things that may or may not happen at all. Anxiety leads to procrastination solely because people are terrified of pushing forward towards the road to success. They come up with many reasons not to move forward because of the negativities circling through their minds. They are provided with multiple reasons why chasing their dreams is a bad idea and there is nothing positive about it.

Anxious people are afraid of going out of their comfort zones because of their fear of failure and committing mistakes, although it doesn't stop there. The minds of the anxious are very wide and wild, so to speak. It starts from their fear of failure and branches out to other negativities. Sooner or later, they will claim their pursuit of success will not only affect their emotional growth but also their families and friends. Even when there is no harm at all, an anxious person will always find a loophole to think that something negative is about to happen.

If you're having this problem and you think this is impeding your ability to get in control, there is no shame in seeking help. When you cannot control your anxiety anymore, visit your nearest psychologist and ask for help. He or she can help you reframe your thoughts into something productive and positive. The psychologist can give you various techniques to use whenever you feel like thinking about something negative.

Depression

Depression is also linked to procrastination. Did you know that depression does not only have a psychological effect but also physiological effects as well? When a person is experiencing depression, it can cause demotivation, sadness, and worthlessness. The worst part is that the mind can signal the body it is in pain even though it is not. This phenomenon, also called 'phantom pain', is very common among depressed patients. When the psychological aspect of a person is in pain, it vibrates towards a person's physiological health, resulting in bodily symptoms such as heartache, stomach ache, loose bowel movement, muscle pain, and fatigue. This causes procrastination and laziness because you will believe that you need more time to rest even if you're not tired at all.

Depression is a very lethal illness that kills millions of people every year. If you're feeling the need to procrastinate all the time, you might as well check your mental status. There is no shame in getting help from a psychologist. He can help you get rid of your depression and get on your way to a productive and successful life.

Emotionality

What is the difference between emotionality and depression? Emotionality is simply one's sensitivity to everything one sees, hears, or smells. When a person is emotional, he is easily triggered by the things around him. He gets emotional over things he should not be sad about. Although there's nothing wrong to empathize and sympathize with other people, without balance, it can cause depression and procrastination. Emotionality is a difficult road to tackle. Most people who are highly sensitive will not admit something is wrong. But when you come to think of the consequences, you're putting yourself in grave danger by overthinking and feeling highly sensitive about all the things happening around you.

We have discussed the power of thought-stopping in the previous chapters. It is inherent that you practice this mind trick to avoid hypersensitivity in various situations. It is also important to start rethinking the reasons for your frustration. Learn to give yourself a pep talk whenever you feel sad about something shallow, distract yourself if possible and use it in a productive way. It will make you feel proud of yourself for accomplishing something and the midst of feeling sad or frustrated.

Low Self-Esteem

The lack of self-confidence is one of the most dangerous causes of procrastination. It makes a person doubt his skills, deeming him worthless to even pursue his dream. When a person lacks a positive self-concept, he is inclined to worry more about what is going to happen in the future. He thinks that he cannot do anything right. Therefore, he prefers to sulk in his couch and do nothing because he cannot accomplish anything anyway.

Self-confidence is a person's belief that he can do anything - that he can face the adversities and trials that life throws his way. Without it, he will think of himself as a lost cause that will curb the moment hardships take control of his life. People without a good sense of self-esteem feels the need to be assisted every step of the way. They feel like they cannot accomplish anything on their own. Without support and care from other people, they feel like they cannot go through with anything. This is common among social loafers. If you have been in a team with mates who do not plan to contribute, the lack of confidence is the real issue, not procrastination. They believe that you are good enough to finish the requirements on your own and their efforts are not needed. They lack a positive self-concept because they believe they cannot do anything right. Instead of being mad at these people for being lazy, uplift their spirits by giving them an activity they will enjoy. Much like how you acknowledge yourself. Think of an activity that you know so much about and start from there. Do not lose hope just because you are afraid to try. When you get started on a job or a task, it is unlikely to stop, especially when you keep motivating yourself to move forward.

Guilt

You might be wondering how guilt can lead to procrastination. Well, there are instances when people feel like they do not deserve such success and self-transformation. There are times when people start to become skeptical when they find out that you have been on the road to self-transformation. A person starts to feel guilty when all of his friends and loved ones keep on saying they liked him better before. The lack of people's support and acceptance can cause guilt. Aside from that, when a person feels like he is missing out on the good things in life, he feels like he is not 'living more'. He'd feel guilty about abandoning his friends and not living life to the fullest.

Perfectionism

Having a high sense of perfectionism is very detrimental to one's productivity. This concept is directly linked to anxiety and depression. Everything has to be in place, on time, and everything must be done perfectly. Whenever things do not go as planned, a perfectionist has two options - to double his efforts or to become demotivated.

When he chooses to double his efforts, he has the tendency to overwork his body and mind, causing mental and physical fatigue. When he chooses to be demotivated, he will be less productive on his goals. Either way, both resort to procrastination, which is why it is important to learn the balance between being too perfect and doing things out of compliance sake.

Unstoppable Day

Try not to expect too much out of yourself and from other people. Remember, you are still trying your best to learn from your mistakes. Do not be afraid to commit one more. Mistakes are vital experiences you can use in your journey to your success.

Do everything the best you can but learn to forgive yourself whenever things do not go your way. There are uncontrolled factors that keep a person from achieving his goals. You need to accept these factors and learn to move on. Everything does not have to go as planned. As long as you are on the right track to success, you should not be worried.

If you keep letting yourself obsess on the verge of perfectionism, you will end up with worse problems within yourself. So, as early as now, learn to have that "I am enough" attitude to prevent any more depression, anxiety, and overthinking.

Expectancy and Value of Reward

The likelihood of getting a reward and the value of the prize either motivates or demotivates an individual to work hard. When a person feels like there is little to no possibility to be rewarded for his hard work, he is more likely to procrastinate and look for another line of work or success. If an individual feel like he has no use for the reward, then he is likely to throw away his tasks for good. But if a person feels like the reward is worth it and there is a high probability for him to receive such reward, he will pursue the tasks with burning effort until he reaches his goal.

I cannot blame you for procrastinating given the low expectancy of reward. But the value of doing things with or without reward is timeless. It is all about the wisdom, skill, and knowledge you learn from your experiences. The most common mistake is assessing the rewards way too much. We need to take every opportunity, be it a small reward or not, to learn from our experiences. If we aim to think about the process rather than the reward, we will be more productive and keener on solving various life problems that challenge our vision.

Delay of Reward

The length of time needed to pursue one's goals is also a factor towards procrastination. This is the most common reason for laziness, especially among students - the due date. When a person feels like the reward is still a long way off, he is more likely to concoct reasons not to do it yet. Phrases like, "I will do it next week or tomorrow" are often said because they believe they still have time to procrastinate. This is a very dangerous path to take. When the brain starts to get accustomed to the thought of doing things later, it is very difficult to condition the mind otherwise. The delay of the reward or due date is one of the reasons why students and workers cram their requirements. They did not expect time to fly by so fast. When they reach the final weeks of rushing their tasks, they start to feel tired and restless.

Unstoppable Day

Hence, leading to lazier hours. Without knowing it, they are doing their tasks only for compliance sake.

As responsible people, we need to stop thinking about the due date and start accomplishing more given the time. Think of rewarding yourself after you have accomplished your tasks. In that way, you can relax, and take your time in doing your work without hassle or rush.

Chapter 11:
Defeat Procrastinating with Your Mind

In the previous chapter, we discussed that the mind is a powerful tool which defines a person's behavior towards his goals. We have tackled that balance is a vital factor in the accomplishment of tasks and the pursuit of success. In this segment, we will be discussing how you can avoid procrastinating before and during the actual completion of a task or activity.

We can observe most of the time that the greatest pull of laziness starts at the beginning of a goal or a task. It is when the body starts to dissuade the mind, reminding it of the hardships and challenges of pursuing the goal. This is the moment of the truth, whether or not you let yourself stay beneath the gravity of procrastination or try your best to pursue success.

The moment before you start your goals is the most deceptive moment of all time. It is when your anxiety, fear, doubts, and depression kick in to meddle on your concentration. To fight this off, you need these eight simple steps to make sure you get out from the black hole and finally start focusing on your goals.

Forgive Yourself for Past Procrastination

One of the most common reasons why a person becomes demotivated is the feeling of not being competent enough. Some would claim they would eventually procrastinate anyway, so there is no use to be as effortful. To move past that thinking, you need to learn how to forgive yourself and forget the times you were weak enough to get sucked in by the dark hole.

Remember, in your morning routine, we discussed the need to think that today is a new day. The past is the past and there is so much to accomplish if you believe in yourself. Whenever you are faced with the challenge of staying lazy on the moment of beginning your task, remind yourself that every day you are trying to become a better person. Beating procrastination is the first step towards your success. Have a little faith in yourself that this time you will not bulge in the midst of laziness. Rather, today you will be more effortful, willing to learn in everything you do.

Redefine What Success Means

It is important to keep reminding yourself of what success looks like. Remember the piece of paper I asked you to write your dreams on in detail? It is time to look at it once again and redefine what it means to succeed. Remind yourself of your reasons why you should be doing these tasks instead of procrastinating. Once you do, you will be more motivated to start pursuing your goals.

Remove Short-Term Distractions

We all have a price that triggers our tempest. For some, it is the television. For others, it is their phones and gadgets. To keep focusing on your tasks for the day, you need to keep out of your temptations. I know you know yourself well enough to determine what entices you to stay lazy. For this goal, I want you to stay away from it. If it is possible to work away from home where there are no distractions, do so. If you want to lose weight, go to the gym where you will be more motivated to push yourself and train.

Learn to Break Your Project into Tasks

Earlier, we have discussed the importance of breaking your goals into smaller tasks and work on that list as you finish. When starting on a new goal, do not think of it as a whole. Learn to break it down into smaller objectives so you will not overwhelm your mind. Simplifying your tasks into smaller ones will trick the mind into thinking the goal is easy to accomplish. It makes you forget to think about the hardships you encounter during the process. And as you work on your list and see the check marks, you will be more motivated to finish it all and feel proud at the end of it.

Redefine Your Tasks as Input-Based

The most common mistake is thinking about what you can accomplish. As a mind trick to get you motivated, think of the experiences and learnings you can acquire from the process. Ask yourself, what should I learn from this goal and how can I apply it in the future? By thinking about this, you will be inclined to perform at your peak, disregarding any hint of hardship because you know this will make you a stronger and wiser individual in pursuit of his dreams.

Set Up the Task.

When starting on an activity, make it a habit to set up your task before you do it. This is the stage where you organize your workstation and prepare everything you need before you get started. In doing so, you can maximize your time and avoid any mishaps of looking for misplaced objects or tools. By setting up the task, your mind is slowly conditioned into performing. Therefore, it is less likely to get stuck in the midst of delay or idleness.

Use Motivational Tools

On your workstation, you can use several apps or DIY's to keep you going. For example, you can maximize the use of your gadgets by downloading apps in the store to help you stay motivated on your goals. Be it a scheduling app or a motivational quotes app, these simple ways can aid you to keep pushing forward despite any difficulties. If not, you can search for a mantra on the internet and write it on a piece of paper. Post it on your desk or your laptop and read it over and over again, especially when you feel the need to procrastinate.

Give Yourself a Break

Lastly, it is important to take short breaks from time to time. This is vital in keeping a strong mind and body to reach your goals. However, remember to set up an alarm to avoid idleness and stagnation. Do not let your mind cool down on the activity. When it does, it kicks in an illusion that the whole body is tired and it needs some rest, which is why you need to keep your mind hot and motivated to make sure it does not get stuck in the black hole. If it is possible to set up an alarm, do so. Give yourself 15 minutes of rest every after an objective. Be sure to never exceed that unless you need more time to eat and prepare more tasks. Keep your brain active whenever you can to avoid putting it into the brink of procrastination.

Chapter 12:
The Growth Mindset Think Long-Term

The details of your success written on the piece of paper symbolize your ability to think long-term. In this chapter, I will discuss why it is more important to think of your long-term goals rather than your short-term ventures. On a more important note, I will be discussing how thinking positively about your long-term goals can help you achieve more and develop more within yourself. With this, I am not saying you should only focus on your long-term goals, but rather explaining how thinking long-term will grant more obvious and worthwhile progress to your success.

Thinking about your short-term goals only defines your accomplishment in a matter of hours, days, or months. Although it is essential to acknowledge your progress in this department for motivation, sometimes, it can bring detrimental effects to your cause. There are instances where focusing on your short-term goals too much can make you overconfident on your abilities. You think that you have learned so much that you no longer need to push yourself further. You decrease your efforts because of the anticipation that the reward is already in the bag. When you uplift yourself too much because of your short-term ventures, there is a huge probability you will limit your willingness to learn and gain experience. Sometimes, a person can get too boastful towards his accomplishments that he no longer feels the need to grow and develop towards real success.

Another disadvantage of thinking too much on your short-term goals is your impulsiveness and impatience to gather the long-term reward. When you think too much about what you have produced for yourself, you start to lose sight of the things you need to learn. All that will matter to you are your accomplishments, degrading your ability to push yourself to the limits. You start to rush your accomplishments and lose sight of what lies beneath that so-called reward. Your outputs become less competent and your thinking becomes stagnant and childish.

On the road to success, you must always remember there are a series of short-term goals to accomplish. You must think of these as a form of training or learning to prepare yourself for more difficult challenges. Look at each of your short-term goals as mere milestones on the road to your real success. As much as possible, stop yourself from being blinded by temporary glory for this can inhibit you from ever growing from your nest. You will start to think that you have reached your success even when you barely made it through half. It makes you greedy and lazy in your future endeavors towards success.

Earlier, we talked about the temporariness of problems. Much like short-term success, they are likely to fade the minute another issue comes in play. Real happiness comes when you have crossed the line. Our long-term goals teach us to stay committed and persistent despite the hardships and trials that life can bring. Because once we have reached the end of the line, we can see how worthwhile our efforts are. We can see how far we have come and we start to appreciate the learnings we acquired no matter how difficult they were to obtain. When we reach our true success, no adversity can destroy our happiness because we have gained the skill and wisdom to get through anything in life.

"Failures, setbacks, bad luck, disasters; they are there to serve you, not hold you back. They toughen you up and drive you to improve. Frustration fuels growth. It gives you the energy and resolve to clean yourself up, get organized, fix what you can, and take the next step."

Larry Weidel

How to Think Long-Term

Develop A Realistic Self-Concept

To learn how to think long-term, you need to start knowing yourself from the inside out. Having a clear picture of who you are allows you to think about where you need to grow and what you need to develop.

If you have a journal, it is crucial to note down the things you want to change about yourself and why it is key to your success. Think about whom you want to be and why you want things to be like that. Acknowledge yourself as a learning individual who is willing to commit to anything that contributes to his development as a person. Once you have determined what you want to change within yourself, it is time to focus on these betterments while breaking down your short-term goals. Learn to link these hardships into something worthwhile like your growth and your dreams.

For example, you are starting to get tired of the things you do to lose weight. Sometimes, you feel like you cannot go any day more. Think about the temporariness of that dreadfulness. Think what you can become if you overcome your thinking. You will become a more disciplined, determined, and committed person. All of which is essential to fulfilling your dreams in the future.

Mistakes Are A Part of Life

Acknowledge the mistakes you commit in your day-to-day. Whenever you do something wrong, let it be a beacon to learning and self-development. Instead of thinking of yourself as a failure, redirect that frustration into something positive like researching on various ways on how you can improve in that department. In lieu of sulking in your bed or the couch and ruminating on your failures, take this as an inspiration to work harder.

First, you need to accept that you have failed. Stop denying yourself the mistakes that you have made. Rather, accept them as a part of the past, and the past alone. Stop yourself from being anxious about further mistakes. Think of yourself as a constructive learner and your mistakes are only setbacks where you can learn more skills and knowledge from. Never forget your values just because you made the wrong move. Think of your life like you are playing chess. Even when you make the wrong move, it does not mean that you have immediately lost the fight. Turn that wrong into a right by making the most of your experience and doubling your efforts to turn that move into your opponent's checkmate.

Reflect on Your Actions Every Day

Before you go to bed, rethink your actions and see how you feel. You can label your behavior as positive or negative, but you should never let these dissuade you or demotivate you into pushing yourself to grow. Whenever you feel like you did something bad, reflect and learn from your actions. This defines how you will deal with more problems in the long run. When you are able to humble yourself and accept your mistakes, it means you are becoming a more responsible person who is willing to learn from his experiences. It means you are starting to feel responsible for your actions and you are willing to do whatever it takes to utilize your mistakes into something right or productive.

Consciously Practice the Thinking

IF YOU ARE used to thinking about the rewards and setbacks of the short-term, try to control your mind by redirecting it to your long-term on purpose. Instead of thinking short-term, ask yourself what you can learn from these challenges in the long run. How can it affect your dreams? Does it let you grow as a more mature person? You have full control of your brain; you just need to learn how to utilize its efforts to think. You can start by reciting your own mantra every time you feel the need to focus on your short-term goals. Or better yet, give yourself time to meditate every day for at least 15 minutes just to allow yourself to think of your long-term goals. You can soon observe the wonders it can bring to your performance and growth.

Work Your Way from Your Needs

It can be very difficult to accomplish your goals with physical and security needs. This usually happens to people who belong to the lower portion of the financial triangle. How can they reach their success if they cannot even have enough money to buy their primary needs? Well, you will be surprised that some of the most successful people in the world came from the bottom of that triangle. They started out as garbagemen who did not even have primary education. But that did not stop them from reaching their dreams.

As they were dealing with their financial constraints, they never lost sight of their goals. Yes, it took time for them to reach their dreams but their goal never stopped when they solved their financial problems. Truth is, that was never their dream. It was only a setback they

Unstoppable Day

needed to solve to stay on track with their long-term goals. So, even when you have primary needs, retain your focus on the things that matter more – your long-term dream. No trial can stop you from accomplishing success as long as you give yourself the chance to develop self-discipline, commitment, and persistence towards your dreams.

Chapter 13:
Shape Your Future

The road into shaping your future is not a walk in the park. There will always be twists and turns, ups and downs, and tops curves, but this should not stop you from living the dream. One of the most important factors that define a person's journey to success is his support system. In this chapter, I will outline how a stable support system can help you accomplish your dreams.

In the previous chapters, we have tackled the downside of having unsupportive friends and family. They can dissuade you from establishing a concept towards self-transformation and success. Plus, they can cause pain and demotivation that can detract your focus from your goals. But this time, I want you to learn the importance of surrounding yourself with helpful people who can assist you on the road to success.

Alleviate Your Feelings

In our darkest moments, having a good friend or family around is very helpful to help us alleviate our feelings of stress, pain, frustration, anguish, and sadness. They are always willing to lend an ear just so they can listen to our problems and try to solve them with us. If you have at least one person to tell everything to, you are lucky. Nowadays, it is very difficult to find someone trustworthy. Your friends and family will always be there to uplift your spirits no matter how difficult it may be sometimes. They boost our self-confidence because they make us feel that we are the best and we can reach our dreams if we wanted to. Our loved ones alleviate our negative feelings and help us ward off the onset of anxiety and depression. They take care of us whenever we fail and they make sure we get back on our feet to start a new day. When you have friends and family around to listen, it can do wonders to your self-regard and persistence to move past your mistakes.

Our Loved Ones Motivate Us

Whenever we feel like we are about to give up, they never fail in providing us reasons to feel inspired. Our loved ones are always there to get us back up on our knees and continue our venture forward. They would never let us back down because of a setback no matter how hard blown it is. Instead, they ready themselves in reminding us about our dreams and aspirations. They never neglect to tell us how amazing and competent we are. Our loved ones make us strong in their own little ways. By just a simple hug or a sentiment, they can make our blood flowing and our minds thinking on the road to success.

They Push Us to Our Limits

Nobody believes more in our capabilities than our friends and family. They know exactly what we can do, sometimes even more so than ourselves. We are lucky to have the few people who are always there to support our endeavors by pushing us to our limits and assuring us everything is going to be okay. They serve as our foundation because no matter how much we fail or commit mistakes, they will be there for us. They show us that they are willing to help us get back out there even when we fail. Our real friends and family are the only people who accept us for who we are despite how hard-headed we might seem sometimes. All they want to see is for us to keep moving forward despite all the hardships because they know that is where we can learn, grow and develop ourselves.

They Give Timely Advice
When we are with trusted families and friends, it is important to share our future or long-term goals. In that way, they can help you evaluate your priorities and your objectives to have better tasks and timeframe on the road to success. The sayings of our parents and elders are timeless. They never go out of hand. As you venture in your road to success, there will always be words from your parents and friends you will never forget. And when the time comes, you will feel lucky to have listened to their advice.

They Push Us to Be Better People
Your real friends and family will support your decisions, especially when it is for self-discovery and success. Your real friends will

always be supportive of your decisions even if it means laying low from your past habits and gimmicks. When they understand your goals and dreams, they will push you towards them rather than inhibiting your growth. They will not try to pull you back to the dark side or criticize your efforts because, as real friends and family, they want nothing but the best for you.

How to Find Better People to Support You

Let's face it, for some people it can be very difficult to have friends and family who can be helpful in achieving their goals. For this reason, you need to look for people whom you can trust. They might be difficult to find, but not impossible. If you live alone, you can join clubs or groups with hobbies that interest you. You can join the book club, chess club, and many more. If you are on the road to weight loss, you can socialize in the gym and look for worthwhile people to be your friends.

But before you disclose your secrets and dreams to people, you need to assess whether they are trustworthy or not. Do not blurt out your secrets on the first day. Build into it and see if they can accept you or not. You can also stay socially active through sports and traveling. You can meet and get to know other people who can help you develop your skills in the future. Remember that everybody has their own background and beliefs. You can learn a trick or two from the people you meet; you just need to be patient when making friends.

If you are trying to retain your old friends, make them understand what you want in life. If they accept you, then great, you can share your goals with them and ask for help. If not, it could be painful, but you need to move on and start surrounding yourself with more positive people.

For people who have difficult families, it is important to try to reach out to them. Make them see you are trying to change. If they accept you for who you are and what you want to be, you can tag them into your goals and ask for help or advice. On the other hand, if they cannot accept you for your dreams, then you are better off looking for support from someone else. When you start to surround yourself with people who believe in you and choose to see your good side, you can observe the wonders it can bring to your life, especially on the road to success. Not only will you have someone to support you, but you will also have someone to fill your life with positivity and ward off any sign of regret, pain, or frustration that might derail you from your goals.

Chapter 14:
Eat Something You Hate

Finally, on the road to self-discipline, I have one more challenge for you. It is to eat something you hate. You may be wondering how can doing something you do not like make you a better person. Simply put, doing something you hate can make you learn new things out of the ordinary. It pushes you to go out of your comfort zone and try something that will make you see and realize things you never thought you could learn. Do you know why humans are disinhibited to try new things? It is because of their mind's stubbornness. Remember when we were children and we did not like to eat vegetables? The only reason why we cried our eyes out was to avoid their taste. It has been ingrained in our minds that it is not good to taste vegetables. It could be through one bad experience like tasting okra and not wanting its slimy texture or our stubbornness could be from other people's experiences. Some would say they have tried it and they never liked it one bit. But remember, we all have differences. It does not mean you will automatically dislike it as well.

In this final segment of the book, I will teach you to live a little more by eating something you hate. And as you progress, I want you to try something that you hate – any activity. Of course, the main problem for this is that our brains are accustomed to the thought that trying new things can be dangerous to our health. Our brains are used to feeling terrified of doing something they are unfamiliar with because of the consequences. Sometimes, we get disgusted at the thought of doing certain activities. We get dissuaded by just thinking about the first step. Little do you know that your potential is maximized by trying new things in life. You learn new lessons. You get stronger. You can overcome your phobia. And most importantly, it will make you feel more alive than ever. I am sure that you do not want to live your life with regret. If you do not do these things now, you are left with the most dangerous question, "What if?" But if you tried your best to get through the experience -even if you do not enjoy it-, you will be left with the satisfaction of knowing that the activity or food is not for you.

Now, it is time to dare yourself to eat what you hate. Of course, disregard anything without any nutrient value. Our goal for this is to take things off from your bucket list –and of course, furnish your command on your mind and foster self-discipline and commitment. Luckily, the modernization of technology allows us to try foreign foods without traveling at all, so I want you to pick a foreign food for starters. If you want it to be more accessible, you can choose your most hated fruit or vegetable.

Unstoppable Day

If possible, try it out with a friend. You can make it fun by daring each other to try new food. Plus, you can ask your friends or family to keep track of your progress. Ask them to give you a penalty if you are unable to do the activity.

Once you have chosen a food, I want you to face your fear and just cut the food into little pieces if possible. Of course, have water beside you just in case. Come up with a tactic to make it easier to ingest, like putting flavorings or seasonings. If it smells bad, it is your choice whether to cover your nose or not. What matters is that you experience its taste. Once you have put the food in your mouth, try to enjoy it even if you do not like the taste. After every spoon, reward yourself with nutritious yet delicious food and go again. I know it may sound silly to try things you are unaware of, but you never know if you will ever like it if you do not try.

This challenge goes hand in hand with trying an activity that you do not like. In this way, you can learn more skills and healthy habits that can aid you on the road to success. For your next challenge, I want you to pick an activity you fear or dislike and have some friends and family accompany you. In trying new activities, tread carefully and ask for assistance from experts. You would not want to get injured by trying it without proper knowledge and equipment.

For this activity, I want you to push yourself and accomplish the task. It does not matter if you fail or succeed. What matters is that you develop your willpower and command to push your mind and be open to more experiences. These small things you do to empower yourself can work wonders for your life. Who knows, maybe that one hateful thing you resent doing will push you towards your greatest desires. Maybe that one experience will bring you the hobby of a lifetime. See, you will never know what you can find at the end of the line unless you try.

If you are doubtful, you might as well think of what you can achieve by doing so. What kind of person will you be after the process? How can this affect you in reaching your long-term goals? See, with a little positivity, you can achieve things unknowingly. You can push your mind to stay committed, persistent, and determined. Once you have acknowledged your ability to gain control of your mind, only then can you have unstoppable self-discipline that will lead you straight to your success. You only live once to let these little moments pass. Remember, no one has conquered success by letting fear stop them at every step of the way.

Conclusion

Turning pro is a mindset. If we are struggling with fear, self-sabotage, procrastination, self-doubt, etc., the problem is, we're thinking like amateurs. Amateurs don't show up. Amateurs crap out. Amateurs let adversity defeat them. The pro thinks differently. He shows up, he does his work, he keeps on truckin', no matter what.

Steven Pressfield

If there is one thing to learn from this book, it is the importance of mind control to overcome all the challenges in life. If you really want to succeed in life, you need to have an unstoppable sense of self-discipline to guide your actions. Without it, you will only keep coming back to your old self – unsuccessful and unwilling to change for the better. In this book, we have discussed the importance of having a well-renowned discipline and how it can affect our other values towards success. Self-discipline is the foundation of all actions towards a person's dream. It guides one's confidence, vision, goals, emotions, and behavior. It governs and defines whether a person will accomplish his goals for the future. It allows a person to obtain helpful habits and morning rituals that can help him or her stay productive despite all the trials in life.

Self-discipline is your weapon against temptation and other forms of enticement. It pushes you to break the cycle that has been holding you back from the road to success. We also established lazy days as inevitable but, with a strong sense of self-discipline, you can find yourself on your desk, ready to accomplish your tasks for the day.

For many years, procrastination has been a part of your habit, inhibiting all hope for you to unleash your potential and progress towards self-hope. Thankfully, all is about to change now that you know how you can vanquish the enemy and avoid the black hole. Never neglect to have confidence, commitment, and persistence. All of these help you build unstoppable self-discipline that can change your life for the better. Not only will self-discipline push you to your limits and help you learn from your experiences, but it can also help you overcome your fears into becoming the next big thing! The power to control your mind easily lies in your willingness to thrive against all odds and grab every opportunity you can to experience more and more. Nobody can live your life better than you do. No one can control your mind and behavior as much as you. Never disregard the power of self-discipline towards your success because it will always serve as your fuel and your drive to a fully-transformed self.

Unstoppable Day

In reading the lives of great men, I found that the first victory they won was over themselves... self-discipline with all of them came first.

Harry S. Truman

Once you have accepted this challenge, you will be ten steps closer to achieving your goals. Your journey starts now. So, get up, look for a piece of paper, and establish your vision to start.

If you find this book helpful in anyway a review to support my endeavors is much appreciated.

Brendon T. Walker

Unstoppable Day

www.ingramcontent.com/pod-product-compliance
Lightning Source LLC
Chambersburg PA
CBHW060454080526
44584CB00015B/1429